FRAMING YOUR WORLD
The Creative Power of the Spoken Word

FRAMING YOUR WORLD
The Creative Power of the Spoken Word

by

Dr. Leroy Thompson, Sr.

Ever Increasing Word Ministries

Darrow, Louisiana

Framing Your World

The Creative Power of the Spoken Word

Second Edition

ISBN 10: 1-931804-33-8

ISBN 13: 978-1-931804-33-2

Copyright © 2001 by Dr. Leroy Thompson, Sr.

Ever Increasing Word Ministries

P.O. Box 7

Darrow, Louisiana 70725

Published by Ever Increasing Word Ministries.

P. O. Box 7

Darrow, Louisiana 70725

Contents

1

Faith's Dynamic Trio

Now faith is the substance of things

hoped for, the evidence of things not seen.

For by it the elders obtained a good

report. Through faith we understand that

the worlds were framed by the word of God,

so that things which are seen were not

made of things which do appear.

HEBREWS 11:1-3

Hebrews 11:3 is a verse you have to read over and over again to get what it is really saying. This verse contains divine secrets concerning wealth and blessing that belong to the born-again believer.

It says, **Through faith we understand that the worlds** [notice this word is plural] **were framed by the word of**

God, so that things which are seen were not made of things which do appear.

Now go back to verse 1: **Now faith is the substance** [invisible, divine substance] **of things hoped for, the evidence of things not seen.**

The *invisible*, divine substance of faith is the substance from which *visible* substances are made. The divine substance of faith—although it cannot be seen with the physical eye—exists and is, in fact, more real than the things that we *can* see. And faith is a more powerful substance too.

Verse 1 says that faith is the substance of things hoped for, the evidence of things not seen. Your faith is always the evidence of whatever it is you're believing God for—whatever it is you're believing to see manifested in your life. Verse 3 says that the worlds were framed by God's own words *spoken*. They were created by the substance of faith.

The invisible world of the Spirit is the realm through which created things, or things we can recognize with our five physical senses, come into being. When we learn how to operate in that realm of creative power, things will begin to manifest in our lives that we heretofore have not thought possible. We are spirit beings—we *are* a spirit, we *have* a soul, and we *live* in a body (*see* First Thessalonians 5:23). There is creative power within us, placed there by God, that will cause those things that we desire in our own world to become a visible reality.

The Limitless Possibilities of God's Word

Did you know that you can frame your world—your situations, circumstances, and your *life*—with the Word of God?

This question has been asked because the Church has not known fully that the Word is authentic, accurate, and unstoppable! There is nothing you can't do if the Word of God is planted firmly in your heart and spoken with confidence from your mouth (*see* Romans 10:8-10). Once you learn how to apply the principles of framing your world with the Word of God, nothing that God has promised—nothing His Word says you can have—shall be impossible to you.

We see in this text in Hebrews 11 that the worlds were framed, or brought into existence, by the Word of God. And we know that it was God's spoken words that accomplished Creation. In Genesis chapter 1, we see the words recorded repeated, "And God *said*...."

For example,

And God said, Let there be light: and there was light.

Genesis 1:3

9

And God said, Let the waters under the heaven be gathered together unto one place, and let the dry land appear: and it was so.

Genesis 1:9

And God said, Let the earth bring forth grass, the herb yielding seed, and the fruit tree yielding fruit after his kind, whose seed is in itself, upon the earth: and it was so.

Genesis 1:11

God is a Spirit, and He used the divine substance of *faith* that was in His word to produce the substance of *manifestation*. (We will look at this topic more in-depth in Chapter 7.)

Hebrews 11:3 says that God framed the worlds with His Word. Another verse says, **Be ye therefore followers** [or imitators] **of God as dear children** (Eph. 5:1). What does it mean to be an imitator of God? It means to copy Him, or to do things like God does them.

God has given us the ability to do certain things like He does them, because He has given us His Word. His Word, the Bible, not only reveals to us God's *will*, but the Word of God is also the *power* of God!

For I am not ashamed of the gospel of Christ: for it is the power of God unto salvation to every one that believeth; to the Jew first, and also to the Greek.

Romans 1:16

As children of God, we are to imitate our Heavenly Father. He framed the worlds with His Word, and we are to frame *our* world with His Word.

You have to go beyond religion to frame your world, because religion will tell you to accept whatever circumstance life throws at you. Religious people will tell you that God is the author of whatever happens to you in life and that His ways are mysterious—therefore, you shouldn't try to understand them.

But God never commended people for not knowing His ways (Ps. 95:10; Heb. 3:10). The truth is, God has revealed Himself to us in the pages of His Word. We must search these things out.

You were born to be a success on this earth. If you have not been enjoying victory and success, you can systematically apply the principles of God's Word and change anything in your life. Success is your birthright! So refuse to be cheated out of it.

I encourage you to underline this phrase or write it down somewhere: *Success is my birthright!* Read and meditate on it over and over again until it becomes lodged in your spirit. If you learn how to properly use the Word of God—as God used it in Creation—it will produce the success of God every time.

God gave you His Word so that you could frame your world. Unfortunately, Christians have been robbed of success because they have been framing their worlds with the wrong words.

Now, don't misunderstand me. A successful life consists of more than material things, a good job, or money in the bank. When talking about success, most people are equating only material things with success. But success with God is a life of total prosperity, in which every need is met in every area of life.

God wants your spiritual walk, your mental and emotional state, your physical health, your relationships, and your financial condition to be successful. But just His wanting it—or even your wanting it—is not enough. You have a greater part to play: You have to frame your world with His Word.

For a long time, many of us in the church did not know that we were supposed to take the Word of God and renew our minds and change our spirit (Rom. 12:2). We didn't know that we were supposed to speak like God speaks—and that those things we say according to God's Word have to come to pass because we say them and keep on saying them (*see* Hebrews 10:23).

Anything in your life that you want to change, the Holy Spirit will help you change it. However, just wanting to change is not enough, because *everyone* wants a change in some area of his or her life. But change will not happen automatically.

To change something in your life for the better, you will have to take the Word of God and frame your world—your situation, circumstances, and surroundings to conform to God's pattern and design as laid out in His Word. You can have your heart's desires if you will heed this message. It may sound too good to be true, but it *is* true—and it will become true for *you* if you'll act on it.

Have God's Faith

Framing your world with the Word of God entails developing yourself in the faith of God.

Mark 11:22 says, **...Have faith in God.** In other words, we can have God's faith. You must know that God's Word is synonymous with faith. Faith comes one way—by hearing the Word of God again and again (Rom. 10:17). You have to develop faith in God—in the Word of God—if you are going to frame your world successfully. You can't do it just by having faith in His Word *unless* you understand that God and His Word are one. In other words, when you have faith in God's Word, you have faith in God's capabilities. Without that kind of faith, you cannot please God (Heb. 11:6).

How are we to imitate God's faith, or "have the faith of God"? The following verse tells us.

> **For verily I say unto you, That whosoever shall say unto this mountain, Be thou removed, and be thou cast**

13

into the sea; and shall not doubt in his heart, but shall believe that those things which he saith shall come to pass; he shall have whatsoever he saith.

Mark 11:23

You can't talk about faith without talking about *believing*. Neither can you talk about faith without talking about *saying*. Did you notice that in Mark 11:23, Jesus mentions the word "say" in some form three times? I think Jesus is emphasizing *saying* over *believing* because that's where people have the biggest problems. They are framing their worlds with the wrong words.

Somewhere along the way, you have been saying with your mouth and agreeing with your heart the things you're seeing in your life today. The good news is, if you don't like what you see, you can turn it around! You can take Mark 11:22 and 23, feed on these verses over and over again, and work them in reverse! Instead of saying things, such as, "That's just my luck—I knew that wouldn't work out," "I knew something would go wrong because it always does," or "I can never get ahead; something always pulls me back," you can boldly and confidently say, "I have faith in God, and I can have what I say!"

The Scripture plainly says we shall have in life what we say: **...he shall have whatsoever he saith** (Mark 11:23). The things that are messed up in our lives are largely the result of our "loose" talking. Our words spoken forth produced the things we spoke. This is the truth Jesus is trying to get over to us: We can use the Word of His power to speak forth *good* things and frame our world with the Word.

Let's look once again at our main text, Hebrews 1:3:

Through faith we understand that the worlds were framed by the word of God, so that things which are seen were not made of things which do appear.

If we were to apply this text to our lives personally, we could say it like this: "We can frame our lives with the Word of God."

This book was written to show you how to do just that.

As Easy as 'ABC'!

There are three simple things you need to know to frame your life with the Word of God: (A) how to *think* right; (B) how to *believe* right; and (C) how to *speak*, or *confess*, right. In a nutshell, these are the ABC's of how to frame your world with the Word of God.

However, for these three principles to work in your life, you must learn to apply them in sequential order. You must think right in order to believe right. And you must believe right in order to confess right.

Likewise, if your *thinking* is wrong, your *believing* will be wrong. And if your believing is wrong, your *confessing* will be wrong too.

Also, if any of these three principles of *thinking, believing,* and *confessing* isn't working correctly, instead of health, you're going to get *sickness*; instead of wealth, *poverty*; and instead of joy, *tribulation.*

The Bible says that death and life are in the power of the tongue (Prov. 18:21). But your tongue will not work by itself! Your mind and heart (your thinking and believing) go before the tongue and influence what it speaks forth! Whether bad or good—whether death or life—the words that come forth from your tongue are the result of what you've been thinking and believing.

Some people readily accept God's Word as truth when it comes to trying to receive something from Him. But they don't accept it as readily when it comes to parts of the Word that talk about having a pure heart that's void of offense, envy, strife, condemnation, and so forth.

Too many people are "putting the cart before the horse." They're trying to run off after hearing a few faith messages, just confessing a bunch of stuff before they get their thinking and believing straightened out.

You must get your *thinking,* your *believing,* and your *speaking* right to enjoy success from the Word as God intends. These spiritual principles of thinking, believing, and speaking will change anything in your life that needs to change. And if you will apply yourself to the Word, it doesn't have to take years to do it!

When you start thinking, believing, and speaking right, you are going to stop certain forces that were working against you. In the past, you were cooperating with those forces through your wrong thinking, believing, and speaking. But those forces will be stopped dead in their tracks when you turn on them with the Word!

For example, when your thoughts are honed into and locked into the truth, deception and lies cannot gain your cooperation. Those thoughts can no longer perpetuate their destructive force in your believing and speaking. Your life will be set on a new course—a course of victory instead of defeat!

As I said, if you *think* wrong and *believe* wrong, your *confession* will be wrong. But if you think right and believe right, your confession will be right, and power will be made available for you to frame your life as God intends.

Do you want a better life? Do you want to live better than you've been living? Then you must learn to *think*, *believe*, and *speak* the Word of God. Your present condition was shaped by the beliefs, thoughts, and words of your past. If you don't like where you are in life, or if you simply want to improve your condition, you can change it. You can learn to change what you've been thinking, believing, and saying—and frame your world with the Word of God.

Not Just Positive Thinking

The first principle for shaping your world is *thinking on*, or *thinking in line with*, the Word of God. Thinking has to do with your mind. To be successful in life, you need to know how to think correctly—how to think the thoughts of God. You have the ability to think God's thoughts, because His thoughts are recorded in the pages of His word.

Some people have gotten confused when they read Isaiah 55:8,9. They said, "See, we can't think God's thoughts."

For my thoughts are not your thoughts, neither are your ways my ways, saith the Lord.

For as the heavens are higher than the earth, so are my ways higher than your ways, and my thoughts than your thoughts.

But these verses were addressed to wicked people. They deal with pardoning the wicked, or the wicked-minded, who repent and look to the Lord for mercy. Look at verse 7: **Let the wicked forsake his way, and the unrighteous man his thoughts: and let him return unto the Lord, and he will have mercy upon him; and to our God, for he will abundantly pardon.**

We have the ability to think God's thoughts, or He never would have commanded us, **...be not conformed to this world: but be ye transformed by the renewing of your mind, that ye may prove what is that good, and acceptable, and perfect, will of God** (Rom. 12:2). We not only have the ability to think God's thoughts, we also have the ability to speak His words in faith and receive heavenly results!

So when I talk about the mind, I'm not just talking about *positive* thinking (although the message of God's Word is certainly positive)—I'm talking about *Word* thinking!

The Blessing of Believing

The second principle for shaping your world is *believing* the Word of God. Believing has to do with your heart, your spirit. You are a *thinking* spirit, a *believing* spirit, and a *speaking* spirit. God is your very own Father, and you are His very own child. Do you believe it?

There are many promised blessings in the Word connected with a person's believing. For example,

> **Jesus said unto him, If thou canst believe, all things are possible to him that believeth.**
>
> **Mark 9:23**

19

> For God so loved the world, that he gave his only
> begotten Son, that whosoever believeth in him should
> not perish, but have everlasting life.
>
> John 3:16

> For I am not ashamed of the gospel of Christ: for it
> is the power of God unto salvation to every one that
> believeth; to the Jew first, and also to the Greek.
>
> Romans 1:16

> Wherefore also it is contained in the scripture,
> Behold, I lay in Sion a chief corner stone, elect, precious:
> and he that believeth on him shall not be confounded.
>
> 1 Peter 2:6

> Who is he that overcometh the world, but he that
> believeth that Jesus is the Son of God?
>
> 1 John 5:5

And, of course, we know one of the classic texts on faith, or believing: ...**whosoever shall say unto this mountain, Be thou removed, and be thou cast into the sea; and shall not doubt in his heart, but shall believe that those things which he saith shall come to pass; he shall have whatsoever he saith** (Mark 11:23)!

Make Your Lips Do Their Duty!

The third principle for shaping your world is *speaking* the Word of God. As we've seen, these three principles go together: *thinking, believing,* and *speaking,* or *confessing.* You are what you are and where you are today because of what you *thought, believed,* and *said* yesterday. It's a spiritual law by which you can accomplish the impossible. Glory to God!

Some people don't want to accept that fact that wherever they are right now, their own thinking, believing, and speaking brought them to that place.

Some people refuse to let go of the past because someone wronged them, and it negatively affects their ability to receive from God. But it doesn't matter if someone wronged you. You are still responsible for how you operate these spiritual principles. If you really want to change your circumstances or the condition you're in spiritually, mentally, or physically, you must change your *thinking, believing,* and *speaking.* There is no other way.

It sounds simple, but there are so many temptations and offers to go another route. Too many people are trying to change their lives a different way. They're rehearsing the problem over and over, thinking that will somehow resolve it.

If that describes you, stop calling things as they are, or as you see them. Stop agreeing with the way things are, but call those things that *be not*—things you want but can't see—as though they were (*see* Romans 4:17). Once you make that call, the things you call for will begin heading your way. Only you and your wrong thinking, believing, and speaking can keep them from coming to you. So learn to *think right* by renewing your mind with the Word, to *believe right* by choosing to believe that every Word God speaks is true, and *speak right* by making your lips do their duty!

Romans 4:17 says that God **…calleth those things which be not as though they were.** It doesn't say He "calleth those things which *be* as though they *were not*"! Faith in God's Word is not the denial of circumstances. It is a belief in God's power to subdue circumstances! Faith is of the heart.

You have to understand that you *are* a spirit, you *have* a *soul*, and you *live in* a body. First Thessalonians 5:23 bears witness to this truth:

> **And the very God of peace sanctify you wholly; and I pray God your whole spirit and soul and body be preserved blameless unto the coming of our Lord Jesus Christ.**

The Bible also says that the outward man (the body) perishes, but the inward man (the heart or spirit) is renewed day by day. (2 Cor. 4:16.) That inward man that is renewed day by day is your born-again, re-created spirit.

You are a spiritual being, created in God's image. Certainly, your mind is involved in framing your world, but in the face of sickness and disease, just telling yourself that you're not sick is not going to work. It might work to a certain degree, but when the devil attacks, if all you've got is *head* faith instead of *heart* faith, he's going to "eat your lunch!"

Heart faith is different. If you have in your spirit the Word of God, which tells you that by Jesus' stripes you were healed (1 Peter 2:24), then with a renewed mind and a robust faith, you can declare that you're healed, and the power of God will back you up and produce healing in your life!

You can summon or subpoena anything from the Word that you desire in life. But you're going to have to think right, believe right, and confess right—not *some* of the time, but *all* of the time. So let go of the jokes and casual talking and get busy framing your world with God's Word!

A Divine Transaction

Romans 10:17 says, **So then faith cometh by hearing, and hearing by the word of God.** When you hear the Word, a divine transaction takes place. *First*, you hear the Word of God. *Second*, the Word goes into your spirit. *Third*, your spirit talks to your mind and renews it with the Word you've heard. *Fourth*, after your mind becomes renewed with the Word, your mouth can bring forth the right confession. You will be on your way to framing your world with the Word of God!

To frame your world with the Word of God means to fashion your life after God's pattern. It means putting your life in order with God, bringing peace and contentment to your life, and becoming equipped to fulfill the intended purpose of God.

You *can* fashion your world after God's pattern. You *can* put your life in divine order. You *can* equip yourself to fulfill the plan and purpose of God. You do it with the Word.

That's how God framed the worlds. Our main text, Hebrews 11:3, says,

> **Through faith we understand that the worlds were framed by the word of God, so that things which are seen were not made of things which do appear.**

God operates by speaking forth words. What kind of words does God speak? He speaks words of faith. So in this Scripture we find a powerful revelation: God made the worlds by faith.

You can read the account in Genesis 1 and see that God indeed framed the world by speaking it into existence. For example, as we already read, God said, "Let there be light," and there was light (Gen. 1:3).

Create Your World by Faith!

By that same principle and method of speaking words of faith, you as a believer can create in your life the things that you want—the things God wants you to have.

It's so simple that most people miss it. They're trying to "pray it through." They're trying to be good enough.

But it's not your goodness and ability that enable you to speak words of faith and frame your world. It's God's goodness and His ability. When you speak His Word in faith, you put His ability to work on your behalf.

The way God created this world is the pattern He has given you as a believer to create, or frame, your own world. To frame your world, you first have to know that you can. You can set your life in order and align it with God's will, which He has laid out for you in His Word.

God will be there to bring every situation in line with His Word if you cooperate with Him—in other words, if your thinking, believing and speaking are right.

You might be thinking, *It's impossible to have every situation in life turn around for good.* But the Bible says, **The things which are impossible with men are possible with God** (Luke 18:27). So when you are applying God's Word to your thinking, believing and speaking, the God of possibilities is with you in every situation.

The faith of God brings you into a supernatural realm in which you can call those things that be not as though they were (Rom. 4:17). But if you begin looking at the situation or circumstances, it may seem as if nothing is happening. That's why your thinking, believing and speaking must be solidly grounded on God's Word—so that through patient endurance, you can hold fast to your confession of faith without wavering.

You see, once you've believed God's Word in your heart and you've confessed it with your mouth, though the physical manifestation takes time, it's already happening in the spirit world.

The worlds were framed first in the spiritual realm, then in the physical realm, by the Word of God. Second Timothy 3:16 says, **All scripture is given by inspiration of God, and is profitable for doctrine, for reproof, for correction, for instruction in righteousness.** That means God breathed all Scripture into existence. Those men who penned the Bible did not write as *they* wanted to, but as *God* wanted them to. Another scripture says, **Holy men of God spake as they were moved by the Holy Ghost** (2 Peter 1:21).

When you think about, believe, and speak the Spirit-breathed Word of God until you are fully persuaded that it is true in your life, it will reshape your world to conform to God's perfect design.

You Must Become Fully Persuaded by His Word

Let's look at Abraham, a man who learned to frame his life with God's Word.

> **Therefore it is of faith...to the end the promise might be sure to all the seed; not to that only which is of the**

law, but to that also which is of the faith of Abraham; who is the father of us all,

(As it is written, I have made thee a father of many nations,) before him whom he believed, even God, who quickeneth the dead, and calleth those things which be not as though they were.

Who against hope believed in hope, that he might become the father of many nations, according to that which was spoken, So shall thy seed be.

And being not weak in faith, he considered not his own body now dead, when he was about an hundred years old, neither yet the deadness of Sara's womb:

He staggered not at the promise of God through unbelief; but was strong in faith, giving glory to God;

And being fully persuaded that, what he had promised, he was able also to perform.

Romans 4:16-21

God had promised Abraham that he was going to have a son. It was a promise that Abraham was going to need to hold on to because his circumstances didn't match up: He was one hundred years old, and his wife was ninety.

In the end, Abraham was fully persuaded that what God had promised him, God "was able also to perform."

Romans 4:19 says Abraham was not weak in faith, so that means he must have been *strong* in faith. Abraham got hold of the ABC's of how to frame his world; and, despite the challenges he faced, he indeed had a son. Verse 18 says Abraham **...against hope believed in hope, that he might become the father of many nations, according to that which was spoken, So shall thy seed be.**

If you get hold of the ABC's of how to frame your world, you can be like Abraham: You can see the fulfillment of the promise of God in your life. You can know without a shadow of a doubt—no matter how it looks or feels, no matter what someone else might be saying—that the Word of God works in your life. When you learn how to apply the Word properly, you'll rise from defeat to victory every time.

2

How To Have the Mind of Christ
Part 1

In chapter 1, I talked about the fact that we are to be imitators of God. (Eph. 5:1.) Since we are to be imitators of God, we are to be imitators of Jesus, too, because He and the Father are one. (John 10:30; 14:9.)

Let's look at another verse of Scripture which is comparable in content to these:

Let this mind be in you, which was also in Christ Jesus.

Philippians 2:5

What kind of mind did Jesus have? Jesus had the mind of God. He thought as God thought. Through Jesus' ability to think in line with God, Jesus believed as God believed. And since Jesus believed as God believed, He was able to speak as God spoke—and He was able to get the results that God got!

The Mind of Christ Defined

What is the mind of Christ? Whatever words were spoken by Jesus in the Gospels were words that expressed His mind. When the five thousand needed to be fed and the disciples had no bread, Christ's mind was that He could talk to the Father, give Him thanks and receive enough food to feed the hungry.

When the two sisters, Mary and Martha, wept because their only brother, Lazarus, was dead and buried, Christ's mind was that He could call him forth from the grave.

Jesus defied natural laws, death and devils. That was the mind of Christ. And the mind of Christ was also knowing that His needs would always be met. Jesus wasn't broke because, when it came time to pay His taxes, Christ's mind was that He could direct Peter to go grab the first fish he could catch, and he would find enough money in that fish's mouth to pay His taxes and Peter's too.

You Must Agree With God's Word in Your Thinking, Believing, and Speaking

So, as believers, we are to have the mind of Christ. What produces that mind in us? The mind of Christ is produced in us first by our hearing the Word of God and letting it become implanted in our heart. Then our heart, which is our spirit, speaks to our mind, and our mind is renewed with the Word so that we can think as Christ would think. Then we can begin to confess and come into full agreement with what God says we are. We can begin to say the same thing that God says about us. That is confession which is based on the Word of God.

This kind of confession is simply agreeing with God. In other words, whatever God says I am, that is what I am, and that is what *I'm* going to say. Whatever God says I can do, that is what I'm going to say I can do. I'll talk more about confession in another chapter, but notice that this kind of confession has nothing to do with feelings. You can't always go by your feelings and agree with God at the same time.

Notice, too, that this kind of confession—confession that is based on the Word of God—has nothing to do with your failures. You cannot constantly think about, dwell on and talk about your failures, weaknesses and shortcomings and at the same time agree with God.

Certainly, if you've sinned, you need to ask God to forgive you. And when you do ask Him to forgive you, He forgives you and He forgets that you've ever done anything wrong (1 John 1:9; Isa. 43:25). So don't go digging into your past mistakes. Don't go looking for things in your life to use to condemn yourself. Just agree with Him by accepting His love and forgiveness.

Forget Feelings and Failures, and Focus on Faith!

As I said, you can't dwell on your failures and agree with God. At the same time, some people won't use their faith because they feel condemned. They feel they've missed the mark too many times. They think it's their good works or their behavior that can get them something from God. But receiving from God is not dependent on *their* works, but on God's mercy.

Anyone who asks God for forgiveness, no matter what he's done, can be forgiven and washed clean by the blood of Jesus. Because of what God planned and wrought through His great plan of redemption, a person can be completely delivered from every bondage in his life and can enter into a powerful walk with God. But he needs to have the mind of Christ. He needs to constantly renew his mind with the Word of God.

Where Thoughts Come From

It's easy to understand where thoughts come from when your mind is renewed with the Word of God. If you are born again, the Holy Spirit inside you will speak to your spirit, and He will speak in line with God's Word. All of God's thoughts will line up with His Word.

The devil will shoot thoughts into your mind from the outside. He will constantly make suggestions to you and try to formulate thoughts in your mind that do not line up with the Word of God.

If you don't recognize that fact and know how to deal with Satan's thoughts when they come, you are going to have problems.

A good rule to follow in determining who's talking to you is to understand that anything that is evil is from the devil. And when you receive a thought that's evil, an alarm should go off in you, warning you that it's not from God. Shut down anything that's evil because the devil is the father of evil.

Hindrances To Having the Mind of Christ

As we are told in Philippians 2:5 to have the mind of Christ, we're going to look at four things that can hinder us from achieving that goal.

The First Hindrance: Ignorance of God's Will

The first hindrance to having the mind of Christ is *ignorance of God's will*. People in this category haven't understood fully that it really is God's will that they think like He thinks! The solution to that hindrance is having knowledge of God's Word and rightly dividing the Word of Truth (2 Tim. 2:15). Find out what one verse says in light of other verses in the Bible. Don't simply pull one verse out of its context in a passage and try to build an entire doctrine out of it.

Some people have believed that they *can't* think like God—that they are not able to have the mind of Christ. To support that idea, they quote this verse from Isaiah 55:8: **For my thoughts are not your thoughts, neither are your ways my ways, saith the Lord.**

But as we saw in Chapter 1, they are not quoting that verse correctly; they're quoting it out of context. Let's look at that passage in context. Isaiah 55:6-9 says,

> **Seek ye the Lord while he may be found, call ye upon him while he is near: let the wicked forsake his way, and the unrighteous man his thoughts: and let him return unto the Lord, and he will have mercy upon him; and to our God, for he will abundantly pardon. For my thoughts are not your thoughts, neither are your ways my ways, saith the Lord. For as the heavens are higher than the earth, so are my ways higher than your ways, and my thoughts than your thoughts.**

Again, who was Isaiah addressing in these verses? Verse 7 says, **Let the wicked forsake his way, and the unrighteous man his thoughts.** Notice it *didn't* say, "Let the *born-again person* forsake his way, and the *righteous* man his thoughts." It said the wicked and the unrighteous.

Then the Lord said in verse 8, **For my thoughts are not your thoughts** [the wicked, unrighteous man's thoughts]**, neither are your ways** [the wicked, unrighteous man's] **my ways.**

God was not talking to the saints, the Blood-bought Church of the Lord Jesus Christ. He was talking to the wicked. He was reprimanding them, telling them to forsake their own wicked, unrighteous thoughts and ways. Isaiah told them in verse 7, **Return unto the Lord, and he will have mercy upon him; and to our God,**

for he will abundantly pardon. In a sense, he was telling them to have the mind of Christ!

Are you wicked? Are you unrighteous? You may have been taught that you are even though you are born again. But if you've been born again, you're righteous. You are the righteousness of God in Christ (2 Cor. 5:21). It's not *your* righteousness; it's *God's* righteousness.

Reading Isaiah 55 and other Old Testament Scriptures incorrectly can blow you right out of the water and keep you from receiving what belongs to you in Christ and what God wants you to have. But we are not wicked. We're not sinners clothed in filthy rags of unrighteousness. We're not beggars trying to get a piece of bread. In fact, in Christ, we're in the baker's shop! It's true that our own righteousness is as filthy rags (Isa. 64:6), but we are not righteous in ourselves. We are the righteousness of God in Christ!

I *was* wicked but, thank God, I'm not wicked anymore! I have forsaken my old ways, and now I operate in God's ways. I *was* unrighteous, but I met a Man called the Righteous One. I accepted Him as my personal Savior, and He gave me His righteousness.

God's Will Is To Forgive and Forget

Don't let the things in your past—the mistakes, the failures and weaknesses—hinder you in framing your world with God's Word. Certainly those things have to be dealt with, if you haven't already done that. But if you are a Christian, they need to be dealt with according to 1 John 1:9: **If we confess our sins, he is faithful and just to forgive us our sins, and to cleanse us from all unrighteousness.**

In other words, confess your sins to God, receive His forgiveness and then *forget* them! Don't let the devil condemn you. Once you say, "Lord, I'm sorry! I missed it, but I want to get back on track," the devil doesn't have any business condemning you!

Even if you missed it this very day, God loves you and He wants to deliver you *today.* You can forsake your wicked ways *today* because *today* is your day!

Tell Them They're Pardoned!

Then look at what Isaiah 55:7 says the Lord will do once a person has returned to Him: **He will have mercy upon him...he will abundantly pardon.** Instead of *abundantly* we could say *fully.* The Lord will *fully* pardon!

Have you ever heard of an incarcerated man going before a parole board for a hearing to determine whether or not he'll be granted an early release? I was actually present at a parole hearing when the parole board voted to let a man go free. I wish you could have seen the expression on that man's face when he was told he'd been pardoned!

I know of several people who spent time in a penitentiary but who were born again and turned on to the Word of God. They got their thinking straightened out, and a parole board released them. If those types of cases were the only ones those board members saw, they would have to quit their jobs. Most of those men will never go back to the penitentiary. They have forsaken *their* wicked ways to go *God's* way. They've forsaken *their* wicked thoughts to think *God's* thoughts. Life will never be the same again for those men.

Many dear members of the body of Christ have been "doing time," so to speak, because they've been deceived by the devil. They've been tricked into believing that they can't be forgiven and that God doesn't love them anymore. Someone needs to tell them that they're pardoned!

The Second Hindrance:
Failure To Renew Your Mind With God's Word

Romans 12:2 says,

> **Be not conformed to this world: but be ye transformed by the renewing of your mind, that ye may prove what is that good, and acceptable, and perfect, will of God.**

A person whose mind is not renewed with the Word of God won't speak in line with God's Word. Or, if he did try to make the right confession, he would simply be saying the words out of his head. He would just be mentally assenting with the Word. He would be speaking with only a vague sense of conviction. His confession would be rendered null and void, because the power of God is not produced by *head* faith; the power of God is produced by *heart* faith. And heart faith is a result of a renewed mind.

Faith is an all-important subject. Our text in Hebrews 11:3 says, **Through faith we understand that the worlds were framed by the word of God.** Just a few verses later, in Hebrews 11:6 we read, **Without faith it is impossible to please** [God]. We are *saved* by faith (Eph. 2:8), so we can't underestimate the importance of Bible faith.

In charismatic circles, we've heard a lot of teaching on faith, and many people emphasize confession when dealing with this important subject. Confession is important, and you could talk about confession all day long. But if a person doesn't have his mind renewed with the Word of God, his heart and mind are not straight. Therefore, his confession won't be right either. You must have your mind renewed.

Let's look at an Old Testament verse that talks about renewing the mind. Joshua 1:8 says,

> **This book of the law shall not depart out of thy mouth; but thou shalt meditate therein day and night, that thou mayest observe to do according to all that is written therein: for then thou shalt make thy way prosperous, and then thou shalt have good success.**

This verse suggests that we have to get in the Word. It says, **Thou shalt meditate therein day and night.** We are to read, study and ponder the Word of God.

What does it mean to ponder the Word? It means to think on it and to rehash it continually—over and over again—with the goal in mind of depositing it into your heart or spirit.

You can't put the Word into action successfully without making it a reality in your spirit man. If the Word is a reality only in your head or mind, feelings will get in the way of your acting on the Word. But if the Word is real in your heart, you have an anchor to hold you steady when the storms of feelings and emotions try to shipwreck you.

The Word is what will bring you deliverance when circumstances say there is no hope. So stay with God's Word. It is a solid rock that will never let you down.

God wants you to ponder the Word today and then ponder it some more tomorrow and the next day. It's a process. Results don't always come overnight. But if you will stay with the Word, results will come. You'll start out walking with the Word, meditating on it continually. Then you'll begin to run in the Word. And eventually you'll find yourself jumping, skipping and shouting the victory because the Word will be a reality in your heart. It will come alive to you, and you'll know it's working in your life even before you see anything change.

Let's read Joshua 1:8 again:

> **This book of the law shall not depart out of thy mouth; but thou shalt meditate therein day and night, that thou mayest observe to do according to all that is written therein: for then thou shalt make thy way prosperous, and then thou shalt have good success.**

As I said, you can't put the Word into action successfully without first making it a reality in your spirit man. And we know from this verse of Scripture that the way to make God's Word a reality in your heart or spirit is by meditating on it.

Notice it is *we* who have to do the meditating, not God. Then it goes on to say, **...that thou mayest observe to do according to all that is written therein.** After we meditate properly, we'll be able to put the Word into action or, in other words, *do* the Word. But notice again that it is we who have to "observe to do according to all that is written." We have a key part to play in this process.

The last part of Joshua 1:8 says, **For then thou shalt make thy way prosperous, and then thou shalt have good success.** Total prosperity in spirit, soul and body is the Father's desire for every believer. But, again, notice that the believer has a part to play: **For then thou shalt make thy way prosperous, and then thou shalt have good success.**

Did you know that God has done all He's going to do about our prosperity and success? So many times we say, "Lord, do this. Lord, give me that." But the Lord has already made prosperity and success available to us. When Jesus hung on the cross, shed His blood, went into hell, whipped Satan and took the keys of death, hell and the grave, prosperity and success were finalized for us.

Jesus said in Matthew 28:18,19,

> **All power is given unto me in heaven and in earth. Go ye therefore, and teach all nations, baptizing them in the name of the Father, and of the Son, and of the Holy Ghost.**

When Jesus reversed the tug of gravity and took a trip to the right hand of the Father on high, He made His power available to us! And what we do with that power is our responsibility.

Prosperity and success are available to us, but we are going to have to do something in order to obtain them. We are going to have to get our thinking, our believing and our speaking in line with the Word of God. We are going to have to renew our minds. We are going to have to observe to do, or act on, the Word. Then we'll be able to make our way prosperous and have good success.

There is, however, a price to pay which will enable you to get your thinking aligned with God's Word. You'll have to throw away those old religious glasses you've been wearing and stop looking at things through the eyes of religion. You'll have to "break up" with your old way of thinking.

Sometimes getting your thinking straight will mean disagreeing with *your* mama and *her* mama and *her mama's* mama so you can agree with God. If what your family believes doesn't line up with the Word, then what they believe is wrong. Don't misunderstand me. You are to love your family members, but you have to agree with God if you want God's benefits in your life.

The ball is in our court. The responsibility lies with each of us to apply the Word to our lives and to frame our world as God intended. God has done His part. He laid it out for us in Christ's death, burial and resurrection. Now we are going to have to take Him up on it. We are going to have to receive it by faith—by thinking, believing and speaking right, according to His Word.

Proverbs 4:20-22 gives us some more insight into the power of a renewed mind. It says,

> **My son, attend to my words; incline thine ear unto my sayings.**
>
> **Let them not depart from thine eyes; keep them in the midst of thine heart.**
>
> **For they are life unto those that find them, and health to all their flesh.**

The phrases, "Attend to my words," "Incline thine ear unto my sayings," "Let them not depart from thine eyes" and "Keep them in the midst of thine heart" all make reference to the renewing of your mind. And why did the Lord say tell us to do these things? Verse 22 tells us why: **For they are life unto those that find them, and health to all their flesh.**

God's words are life. They will frame your world. They will change your situation. They will put you in a position of victory. But before God's words can become life to you in reality, you have to put them into you, into your spirit. In a sense, you have to eat God's words!

To illustrate that point, a professional athlete has to eat certain foods and train properly in order to perform at peak capacity. He can't just eat sweet rolls, cakes and pies and lie in his hammock if he's going to stay strong. Eating the wrong things and failing to exercise properly will make him weak and inefficient.

Similarly, to frame your world with the Word of God, you're going to have to take in the right "food." You're going to have to take in the food contained in the Word, and you're going to have to exercise your faith. And you have to do it consistently; you have to do it every day. It's not a once-every-Sunday deal.

If you find your life lacking in a particular area, just keep coming to the table to eat of the Word! Continue to exercise your faith. Don't let up, or you won't be ready when the tests of life come.

Jesus said, **Man shall not live by bread alone, but by every word that proceedeth out of the mouth of God** (Matt. 4:4). When the enemy comes against you, if you've been feeding on the Word and exercising your faith, you'll be ready. You'll win the battle. You'll be spiritually strong and able to withstand the opposition.

Some people wonder why their faith is not working. It's because they don't have the whole picture. They might have heard the Word often enough to have it in their heads, but they don't have heart faith working for them.

The Holy Ghost would not tell us to have the mind of Christ if it were not available to us. So, since He told us to have the mind of Christ, we know that the mind of Christ is available. The mind of Christ is found in the Word of God, and God made it available through the process of renewing our minds with His Word. Now it's up to us to see to it that we have the mind of Christ. It's not automatic; it will take effort. We're going to have to work on having the mind of Christ.

The Third Hindrance: Impatience

The *third* hindrance to having the mind of Christ is *impatience*. In other words, some people won't take the time to learn of Jesus and renew their minds with the Word.

> And as for that in the good soil, they are those who, hearing the word, hold it fast in an honest and good heart, and bring forth fruit with patience.
>
> Luke 8:15 RSV

> For ye have need of patience, that, after ye have done the will of God, ye might receive the promise.
>
> Hebrews 10:36

> Come unto me [Jesus], all ye that labour and are heavy laden, and I will give you rest.

> Take my yoke upon you, and learn of me; for I am meek and lowly in heart: and ye shall find rest unto your souls. For my yoke is easy, and my burden is light.
>
> Matthew 11:28-30

Another New Testament verse says, **In the beginning was the Word, and the Word was with God, and the Word was God** (John 1:1). That's talking about Jesus—Jesus is the Word. When you learn of Him, you are renewing your mind.

So in the process of learning of Jesus, you get your mind "fixed" or renewed. People often quote Matthew 11:29, but many don't see the fruition of it in their lives. Jesus said, **Take my yoke upon you, and learn of me; for I am meek and lowly in heart: and ye shall find rest unto your souls.** This verse is saying that if you *learn* of Jesus, you are going to be able to *think* like Jesus. Then Philippians 2:5 will be fulfilled in your life, and you will have the mind of Christ.

3

How To Have the Mind of Christ
Part 2

In review, to frame your world with the Word of God, you've got to do three things: (1) think right, (2) believe right and (3) speak, or confess, right. In order to do these three things, you have to have the mind of Christ. And to have the mind of Christ, you must renew your mind with the Word of God. To renew your mind with the Word of God, you must hear the Word over and over again. You must feed on it and build it into your spirit or inner man.

When You Change Your Thinking, You Change Your Way of Life

When your mind is renewed, you have the mind of Christ and you begin to think as God thinks. You get your old way of thinking straightened out. For example, if your mind is renewed in the area of healing, it's hard to remember a time in your life when you thought divine healing had passed away. It's hard to remember a time when you thought the only way you'd ever receive help for your body was through medical science or some other natural means.

You see, through reading, studying and meditating on the Word of God concerning healing, you get your thinking straightened out, and now you know the truth. You hear the Word of God concerning healing, and eventually you get your mind straight about it. It doesn't happen automatically, and it doesn't happen overnight. But you hear the Word and you keep applying the Word, and then your mind is renewed concerning healing.

I tell you, I don't accept sickness anymore. I didn't say that I don't ever get attacked. I can get attacked in my body just like anyone else. But I have come to know from the Word of God that Jesus died not just for my sins, but for my sicknesses as well. So I appropriate the Word of God for my body, just as I appropriate the Word for my spirit.

If you can trust Jesus for eternal life, you can certainly trust Him for your physical health and well-being! But many people are not in a position to trust Him for healing for their bodies because of a lack of teaching along that line. Others aren't trusting Him for healing because they aren't applying what they've heard. Therefore, their thinking and their believing are not right either.

The Fourth Hindrance: Failure To Cast Down Imaginations

As I stated before, the *first* hindrance to having the mind of Christ is *ignorance of God's will*. The *second* hindrance is *failure to renew your mind with the Word of God*. The *third* hindrance is closely connected to the second hindrance, and that is *impatience*. The *fourth* and last hindrance I'm going to talk about is *failure to cast down evil imaginations*.

> (For the weapons of our warfare are not carnal, but mighty through God to the pulling down of strong holds;) casting down imaginations, and every high thing that exalteth itself against the knowledge of God, and bringing into captivity every thought to the obedience of Christ.
>
> **2 Corinthians 10:4,5**

What does it mean to cast down imaginations? It means to *cast down thoughts*. What kind of thoughts? Every thought that exalts itself against the knowledge of God, against the mind of Christ. Every thought that is contrary to the Bible we are to cast down. We are not to think or dwell on it.

Why are we to cast down evil imaginations? Because if we don't, those thoughts will affect our thinking, our believing and our speaking. Every Christian at one time or another has had to cast down imaginations. Not one of us is immune from having thoughts that are wrong come to us. Those thoughts are coming, so we'd better know what to do about them before they come!

Imaginations and high things will come into your mind and exalt themselves against the knowledge of God. How do you keep yourself free from that? How do you keep yourself in a position where you can think right? Well, look at 2 Corinthians 10:5:

> **Casting down imaginations, and every high thing that exalteth itself against the knowledge of God, and bringing into captivity every thought to the obedience of Christ.**

In the first part of the verse, you're locking out evil imaginations or thoughts. In the second part of the verse, you're bringing those thoughts captive. Captive to what? Captive to the obedience of Christ. In other words, you're bringing them captive to the mind of Christ!

How To Cast Down Wrong Thoughts and Bring Them Captive to Christ

For example, if the devil were to come against you with thoughts, such as, *God told you to do this one particular thing, but you're not able. You can't do it. You'll fall flat on your face,* what are you supposed to do? You're supposed to immediately stop thinking in that vein, and you're to line your thoughts up with the Word. You might say, "Oh, no, I won't fall flat on my face. The Lord upholds me with His hand, and I can do all things through Christ who strengthens me!" (Ps. 37:24; Phil. 4:13).

Or what if the devil were to say to you, *You're not going to make it this time. This need is not going to be met. God is not going to come through for you.* If you were obeying 2 Corinthians 10:5, you would say something like, "God is faithful" (1 Cor. 1:9; 10:13), "Heaven and earth will pass away, but His Word will never pass away" (Matt. 24:35), or "My God will supply all my needs according to His riches in glory" (Phil. 4:19)!

When the devil challenges your faith, you can answer his challenge with the Word. You can cut him off every time with the words, "It is written." You can counter his attack with the Word. You have to rise up and say, "No, Devil. You're lying about that. You're a liar, and the truth is not in you. *You're* the one who's not going to make it. My Father told me that I'm going to make it. In fact, I've already made it. I just have to hook up with what He's already done for me."

When you do that, you are bringing those evil thoughts into captivity. You are capturing them with the Word of God, locking them out of your mind and not allowing them to interfere with the Word of God. You are banishing those thoughts from your thinking. Why? Because if your thinking is wrong, your believing will be wrong. And if your believing is wrong, your speaking will be wrong. And if your thinking, believing and speaking are wrong, you will not be able to frame your world with the Word of God.

You Can't Follow the Crowd and Succeed With God

To successfully frame your life with God's Word, you have to have the attitude that no matter what anyone else says, the Word of

God is right and everything else is wrong. It can't matter to you how it looks or feels, because you're sticking with the Word.

Joshua and Caleb are examples of two men who didn't follow the crowd. In fact, they went *against* the crowd in order to stay with the Word. The other ten spies had a bad report about the land the Lord had promised them. They said, "We can't take that land. There are giants in that land, and we are as grasshoppers in their sight!" (Num. 13:1-33)

But Joshua and Caleb had a *good* report. They brought evil thoughts captive, and Caleb said, "We know what the Lord promised us. We're sticking with the Lord. We are well able to take that land!"

Twelve men were in the same place. They were spying out the land the Lord had already said was theirs. Why did two men see differently than the others? Because they had their minds right! They thought like God thought. They forsook their own thoughts and brought those thoughts in line with what God had said.

To frame your world with the Word of God, you can't be a crowd follower, and you can't be a crowd pleaser. Joshua and Caleb framed their world with the Word of God. They stayed with the Word, and through faith and patience they inherited the promise of God as a result (Heb. 6:12). But the other ten spies, along with thousands of other Israelites, died in the wilderness, never having entered into what God had said was theirs.

Those ten unbelieving spies succeeded in getting the people so upset and afraid that they all refused to bring their thoughts captive to what God had said. They rebelled together, and they all died as a result of it.

I'm not moved by the crowd anymore. If every person I was preaching to in a meeting got up and left the building one evening, I'd show up the next night ready to preach to whoever showed up! I believe God's Word. I have applied it my life, and God has blessed me so much that I can't afford to let what others may think change my mind about the Word.

Joshua and Caleb could have said, "Oh, no! What are we going to do? We're outnumbered ten to two! Maybe the others are right. Maybe we *can't* take the land!" But, no. Joshua and Caleb stayed with the Word.

Stick With the Word, and the Word Will Stick With You!

When you're standing on the Word, there are going to be those who will disagree with you and come against you. They may even say bad things about you. They will call you a religious fanatic. But don't worry about all of that. Just keep on holding fast to your confession or, as Hebrews 10:23 says to do: **Let us hold fast the profession of our faith without wavering; (for he is faithful that promised).**

God's Word will never fail. And when you get to the point where you know that you know that fact is true and you refuse to think anything else but what God has said, you are on your way to framing your world in style with the Word of God!

Sometimes casting down imaginations will mean refusing to listen to what other people say, because sometimes imaginations come through other people's mouths!

You Can Be Stable in an Unstable World

For every high thing that exalts itself against the knowledge of God, we have to make up our minds that we are going to bring those things captive to the obedience of Christ. Whatever Christ says we are to do, that's what we should determine to do.

Now in the unstable world in which we live, we have to have our minds made up that we are going to obey Christ. We have to be "gung-ho" and not "gun-shy!" While the world is being governed by the sense realm—"If it feels good, do it!"—we have to say, "I'm going to believe what God's Word says over what I feel and see. I'm going to walk by faith and not by sight." (2 Cor. 5:7.)

While the world is stepping on others to get to the top, we have to say, "I'm going to follow Jesus and His example. I'm going to walk in love and trust God."

I have reached the point in my life where I don't even mention the things someone else has said to me or done to me. I just say,

"Glory to God, let's roll. Let's go get a hamburger and talk about Jesus!"

Casting Before Confessing

As I said before, many want to emphasize confession when they are talking about faith. That's good and that's right, but confession is only one part of the picture. In other words, you can't neglect your thinking and your believing and just skip over those facets of faith and camp on confessing!

Remember, I said that if your thinking is wrong, your believing will be wrong; and if your believing is wrong, your confessing will be wrong. That's why Paul wrote these words to the church at Corinth (and they still apply to the church today):

> **Casting down imaginations, and every high thing that exalteth itself against the knowledge of God, and bringing into captivity every thought to the obedience of Christ.**
>
> **2 Corinthians 10:5**

We have to do some *casting down* before we can successfully do some *confessing!*

Since the Word of God tells us to cast down imaginations and every high thing that exalts itself against the knowledge of God, then there must be some imaginations and some high things that are going to show up in our lives and come against the knowledge of God. There wouldn't be any reason to tell us to cast them down if there weren't going to be any to cast down.

You Can Pull Down 'High Things'

Let's look in greater depth at the two words in 2 Corinthians 10:5.

> Casting down imaginations, and every high thing that exalteth itself against the knowledge of God, and bringing into captivity every thought to the obedience of Christ.

Now let's look at Ephesians 6:12 to understand more clearly what Paul was saying:

> For we wrestle not against flesh and blood, but against principalities, against powers, against the rulers of the darkness of this world, against spiritual wickedness in high places.

First, notice that we don't wrestle against flesh and blood. What we wrestle with is higher than that. We wrestle with principalities, powers, rulers of the darkness of this world and spiritual wickedness in high places.

Now, anything that puts itself above the Word of God is too high. We have to deal with those high things and let them know that the knowledge of the Word of God is the highest thing that exists. There is no company, corporation, organization, institution, entity, person, place or thing that is higher than the knowledge of God. Jesus said, **I am Alpha and Omega, the beginning and the ending** (Rev. 1:8; 21:6; 22:13).

These principalities and powers in high places will try to influence you. They will put imaginations, thoughts and suggestions into your mind and try to get you to yield to them. But God said to cast down those imaginations, thoughts and suggestions—every high thing that exalts itself against the knowledge of God (2 Cor. 10:5).

So since God tells me to cast these things down, then I must have the ability to do so. Otherwise, God would be unjust and unfair. And we know that God is neither of these things. When wrong thoughts come, I have the ability to reach up by faith in my heart and pull those thoughts down. When those thoughts try to rise up and take a high place in my mind, I tell them, "Oh, no, you don't! Come back down!" And Jesus remains on the throne of my heart and my mind.

The Bible tells us in Second Corinthians 5:7 that we are to walk by faith and not by sight. When we cast down wrong thoughts, we are walking by faith and not by sight or feelings or vain imagination. When circumstances look wrong, when things don't feel right and when rapid-fire thoughts are being fired at our mind, we can make the declaration of faith, "Jesus is Lord!"

We can make Jesus Lord over every situation in our lives. We do that with the Word—by taking every thought captive to that Word. We are commanding that our lives line up with what God has said and not with what things looks like.

It doesn't matter to me if my life appears to be going the wrong way. It's *not* going to go that way if I cast down imaginations and bring them captive to Christ or to the Word. I declare and decree that the Word is true about me and my situation. I believe it, I receive it and I *have* it!

It's not a matter of saying, "Jesus *was* Lord," or "Jesus *is going to be* Lord," or "I'm waiting for the Lord to come back and get us." No, it's a matter of saying with your mouth and meaning from your heart, "Jesus *is* Lord." Yes, I know Jesus is going to come back one day and take over completely, but in my life, He has already taken over.

You don't need to wait for Jesus to come back to be a spiritual giant for Him. You ought to be a faith-giant *right now.* When wrong thoughts come, you ought be saying, *"What* did you say, Devil? *Who* are you talking to?"

I heard another minister say one time that when a wrong thought comes wafting into your mind, you can't just start shooting at it. No, you have to arrest it, handcuff it and *then* shoot it! That is a humorous way to illustrate how to cast down imaginations and bring them captive to the obedience of Christ.

Wrong Thoughts Come to Everyone

Some people believe that if they have wrong thoughts, it means they are bad people. But that's not true. Wrong thoughts come to every one of us. It's what we do with the thoughts that counts. We are to take every wrong thought captive and bring it under the Word of God.

Even while doing something spiritual, you can be subject to having wrong thoughts, or thoughts that steal your attention away from God. For example, you might be praying, and all of a sudden the thought comes to you, *I'm hungry. I believe I'll go out for a bite to eat.* Or you might be studying your Bible and have a thought, such as, *I need to go clean out the garage.*

You can't stop the devil from coming against you with thoughts, imaginations and suggestions when you're in the middle of prayer or Bible study, but you can pull them down every time they come. If the devil says to your mind, *You're sick, and you're not going to get well,* you can say, "No, I'm healed in Jesus' name. First Peter 2:24 says that by His stripes I was healed. I'm already healed, Devil."

Maybe you've been tormented with wrong thoughts. Maybe the devil has told you that you'll never be fruitful in the Word, that you'll never frame your world with the Word of God and be the success in life that He wants you to be. Don't let the devil lie to you any longer. Don't let him tell you that success and happiness from God are for others but not for you. Learn to take those thoughts captive before they destroy you. Rise up and resist the devil with the Word. If you do, James 4:7 says he will flee from you.

So just because you have a wrong thought doesn't mean that you're not a good person. As a matter of fact, the more you try to walk with God, the more wrong thoughts may come at you. The devil has to try to fool you on a higher plane, because now you know the Word. In other words, he can't send any more wimpy thoughts at you like he used to.

The devil doesn't want you to walk closely with God. If you're reading, studying and meditating on the Word regularly, the devil will try to sabotage you, diverting your thoughts from the Lord. He will try to infiltrate your thinking, get you sidetracked and eventually get you *sidelined*.

But God loves you, and He wants you to love Him. He wants you to love Him and His Word so much that you will live it every day. You need to make up your mind today that you are going to get into the Word and be a doer of the Word, casting down imaginations and bringing every single thought captive to what God has said.

You *can* have the mind of Christ. You *can* frame your world, or your life, with the Word of God. You are a winner, not a loser. God created you to win, and He is on your side. So be mindful of God's will through His Word and renew your mind with the Word. Take the time to learn of Jesus so you can think as He thinks, believe as He believes and get the results that He gets!

Last, cast down evil imaginations and make low in your life every high thing that exalts itself against the knowledge of God. Through your knowledge of God and His Word, you can have the mind of Christ and prepare yourself to begin framing your world as God intended.

4

Three Aspects of Casting

In this chapter, I'm going to show you three aspects of casting that would hinder you from having the mind of Christ. I want to show you how to cast *down* thoughts, to cast *out* devils or demons and to cast *upon* the Lord all of your cares and worries.

If you get hold of these three aspects, you'll be on your way to having the mind of Christ so you can frame your world with the Word of God. You'll know exactly what to do when the tides of trouble rise high in your life. You'll know exactly how to handle any situation because you'll have the right things in your mind. Then the wrong things will be cast *down, out* or *upon.*

Casting *Down* Imaginations

I already covered the first aspect in some detail— casting down imaginations or thoughts—but let me show you something else about casting down thoughts. Second Corinthians 10:3,4 says, **For though we walk in the flesh, we do not war after the flesh: (for the weapons of our warfare are not carnal, but mighty through God to the pulling down of strong holds).**

The carnal mind is actively hostile and antagonistic toward the things of God. It has a deep-seated ill will against the knowledge of God. Before a person is born again, he has a carnal mind.

Don't tell me, "Well, I was basically a good person even before I was saved." You weren't good for anything, because if your mind was toward God and the things of God, you wouldn't have been a sinner! You would have been a saint all along.

If the "good" sinner who lives down the street really isn't against the things of God, he would accept for himself the great price Jesus paid for his salvation. But, no, that person has a carnal mind, and he *will* have a carnal mind until the Word of God breaks through and he turns from darkness to light by accepting Jesus Christ as his Savior.

There is no goodness outside of God. The sinner has a carnal mind, and it's as simple as that.

The Carnal Christian Is at Odds With God

Carnality slips in even on Christians sometimes. In the new birth, your mind and your body—your flesh—are not born again. Your spirit is born again, but you need to get your mind renewed with the Word of God. If you don't, you are going to be against the things of God even as a Christian. You will be against Him in your thinking, in your believing, in your speaking and in your actions. And until you *receive with meekness the engrafted Word*, as you are told to do in James 1:21, you will remain carnal and unteachable.

The devil wreaks havoc in the home of a carnal Christian. Something you need to know about the devil is that if he can get any kind of ride into your house, he's going to come in. And he will get in because you let him in. You will open the door either through simple ignorance of the Word or through open consent because you're unteachable, actively hostile and antagonistic toward the things of God.

Christians who do not renew their minds fall right back into carnality. They have ill will toward the things of God. That's why a lot of church folks fight God's Word. They are carnally minded. Sometimes they don't even know what's wrong in their lives. They're just mad—hostile and antagonistic toward the things of God.

Unfortunately the church as a whole is not where it should be. The church should be preaching the gospel, laying hands on the sick and casting out devils. We shouldn't be sitting in the pew singing out of a songbook while at the same time feeling mad at the preacher or a fellow church member. Signs and wonders are to follow believers. Supernatural things ought to be happening in our lives. But that won't happen in the life of a carnal-minded Christian. He needs to have the mind of Christ.

Second Corinthians 10:3 says, **For though we walk in the flesh, we do not war after the flesh.** Well, since we don't war after the flesh, what do we war after? We war after or by the Spirit. Verse 4 says, **For the weapons of our warfare are not carnal, but mighty through God to the pulling down of strong holds.**

Since our weapons aren't carnal, what are they then? They are spiritual. But if we are carnally minded, we can't use the spiritual weapons God has given us in His Word, and we can't war a good warfare "after the Spirit." So we are relegated to simply "getting by" in the flesh, trying to frame our world in our own way. But that will never work if we want God's blessing.

Now let's look again at the words in 2 Corinthians 10:4 and talk about strongholds: **For the weapons of our warfare are not carnal, but mighty through God to the pulling down of strong holds.**

A stronghold is a satanic force that starts as a thought, then lays its foundation in a person's mind, builds itself up and makes its abode there. You can't simply cast down a stronghold as you would cast down an evil thought or imagination. You need the Word of God to become like a hammer in your life in order to tear down that stronghold and get it out of your system.

The Lord Is a Strong Tower

How can you get rid of a stronghold? By having a strong *tower!* Psalm 61:3 says, **For thou [Lord] hast been a shelter for** me, and a strong tower from the enemy. Proverbs 18:10 says, The name of the Lord is a strong tower: the righteous runneth into it, and is safe.

The Word of God can become so strong in your life that it can demolish strongholds. The Lord can become the strong tower in your life, and He can push out that satanic force that's been holding you captive.

A stronghold is strong; that's why it's called a stronghold! But God's Word is stronger. If you give place in your life to the Word, that Word can pull down that stronghold. But you have to give place to the Word. You have to renew your mind and cast down wrong thoughts.

Casting *Out* Devils

Strongholds can grow and turn into demonic activity in a person's life, so you have to know how to deal with the devil. Many believers don't know how to deal with him because they are too busy going from meeting to meeting, following signs instead of having signs follow them! Mark 16:17 states, **These signs shall follow them that believe; In my name shall they cast out devils; they shall speak with new tongues.**

This verse is talking about the believer. Every believer, every child of God, has the authority in the name of Jesus to cast out devils.

Sometimes it's more than just thoughts or imaginations that come against a person. Sometimes a demon spirit tries to oppress him. I'm not talking about demon *possession;* I'm talking about demon *oppression.* The devil can come against a Christian to oppress his mind or his body, but devils or demons can't get into his spirit to *possess* him unless the Christian voluntarily renounces Jesus and lets them in.

If you are being harassed, oppressed or tormented by an evil spirit, you need to know how to take authority over it and cast it out of your thinking. You need to know your authority and say with spiritual boldness and confidence, "I command you to leave now, in Jesus' name!"

You can know on the authority of God's Word that when you tell a spirit to go, it has to go. The Bible says it has to go.

As I said, every believer can cast out a demon. It's nothing to be afraid of. For example, if I knew I was in faith about healing and nothing was happening, I'd check my spirit to see if the Holy Spirit was witnessing to me that an evil spirit was present and hindering the healing. Then I'd say, "I cast you out, in Jesus' name. My body is the temple of God. I command you to leave God's property!" After I did that, I wouldn't worry or be concerned about an evil spirit trying to stand in my way. I'd just continue in faith and expect to see the answer.

One of the signs that should follow the believer is the casting out of devils, but I believe that some churches have become fanatical about it. They're casting devils out every Sunday. They look for demons behind every bush. That's nothing but a trick that the devil has played on the body of Christ to cause them to get off in a ditch on one side or the other of the truth.

There is a middle ground on this issue of casting out of demons. The truth is not in one ditch or the other; it's right down the middle of the road. Everything that goes wrong is not caused by a demon or devil. Sometimes it's the flesh that is the problem. Many times a person is suffering because of a wrong decision he or she has made. The devil had nothing to do with it except maybe to try to influence the person to make the bad decision. So sometimes it is a choice made by the flesh that causes problems.

Then in the ditch on the other side of the truth, some people totally deny the existence of devils or demons. Or if they do believe that demons exist, they refuse to ever talk about the subject. But casting out devils is one of the signs that should follow believers. Mark 16:17 doesn't say that it is a sign for preachers only. It says, **These signs shall follow them that believe.**

If you are a believer, you have within you devil-casting-out power! Now that doesn't mean you can always take authority over demons which are operating in another person's life. I've walked right by some people who were operating under the influence of a demon spirit, and I just kept walking. I went on about my business. Why? Because some people *want* the devils that are operating in their lives. It wouldn't do you any good to try to deal with those evil spirits, because the people are giving place to them. They don't want to have those demons cast out of them.

You have the power within you to cast out devils, but you need to base your confidence on the Word and have a renewed mind in that area. In Acts 19:13-16, the seven sons of Sceva thought they'd try casting the devil out of someone, but it backfired on them, because they were doing it just to be doing it.

> Then certain of the vagabond Jews, exorcists, took upon them to call over them which had evil spirits the name of the Lord Jesus, saying, We adjure you by Jesus whom Paul preacheth.
>
> And there were seven sons of one Sceva, a Jew, and chief of the priests, which did so.
>
> And the evil spirit answered and said, Jesus I know, and Paul I know; but who are ye?
>
> And the man in whom the evil spirit was leaped on them, and overcame them, and prevailed against them, so that they fled out of that house naked and wounded.

The man who had that devil in him jumped on those seven men and "prevailed against them"! I mean, he ripped their clothes off and gave them a whipping! Why? Because they were not connected to the Man, Jesus, and His Word. Remember, Jesus is the One who gives the power to cast out devils. And He has given that power to you and me, as believers.

Make up your mind that you are going to rise up and take your rightful place of authority over devils or demons—evil spirits that would try to come against you to keep you from framing your world. Those wicked spirits in high places want to ruin our lives, and they will if we let them. We need to make up our minds that we're going to think right, believe right and speak right, according to the Word. As it says in Ephesians 4:27, we're not going to give place to the devil.

Casting Your Cares *Upon* the Lord

I've already discussed casting *down* imaginations and casting *out* devils. Now I want to talk about casting your cares *upon* the Lord. First Peter 5:7 says, **Casting all your care upon him; for he careth for you.**

Some Christians have never used this verse, but it is powerful. I've used it countless times, and it has been a blessing to my life. Many times when hell was on my trail and it seemed as if everything that could go wrong was going wrong in my life, I leaned heavily on this simple verse of Scripture. Especially where my ministry is concerned, I refuse to take on the care of running it. Actually, it's not even *my* ministry. God called me, and He put it all together, so I give Him the care of keeping it running smoothly.

Some ministers can't even leave town for a few days without worrying about what's going on at the ministry back home. They call in constantly. Some pastors can't even get through dinner without calling the church secretary to ask a question about something.

I train my congregation and give them the Word. They act right when I am out of town, they give right and they serve right, so I don't worry. And my staff, including my secretary, knows what they are supposed to be doing. I don't have to look over their shoulders and mind their business and mine too!

There's no sense in carrying burdens and cares. It is counterproductive to worry and fret and have anxiety. It doesn't produce anything positive. In fact, it has a negative impact on the situation at hand, as well as on you spiritually. If you're worrying about something, you're certainly not thinking right. And you're not believing right or speaking right either.

If you're going to frame your world with the Word of God, you need to get rid of imaginations, demons and cares. You need to cast down imaginations, cast out demons and cast your cares upon the Lord.

Refuse to be loaded down with cares. I tell you, Christians should not be worried and burdened down. I've already made reference to it, but look at Matthew 11:28,29. It says,

> Come unto me, all ye that labour and are heavy laden, and
> I will give you rest. Take my yoke upon you, and learn of me;
> for I am meek and lowly in heart: and ye shall find rest unto
> your souls.

In Matthew 11:28 Jesus says, "Come unto Me." Many have done that. They've come to Jesus and they've been born again, but they've stopped right there. They didn't continue in their walk with the Master.

What does Jesus say to the one who is burdened or ladened with cares? He says, "I will give you rest." And when you're worrying, it's not rest; it's confusion. But Jesus said He would give you rest.

Well, how do you get that rest? Look again at verse 29: **Take my yoke upon you, and learn of me; for I am meek and lowly in heart: and ye shall find rest unto your souls.**

Let's take this verse apart step by step and examine it. How do you take Jesus' yoke upon you? By hooking up with His Word. If something is not of the Word, you have no business yoking up with it. If you do, it will burden you. It will weigh you down. First John 5:3 says, **For this is the love of God, that we keep his commandments: and his commandments are not grievous.** Another translation says that His commandments are not *burdensome*.

Next, how do you learn of Jesus? We talked about it in the last chapter. You learn of Jesus by learning of the Word, for Jesus is the Word. (John 1:1.) Many don't take the time to learn of Jesus, and it costs them. They aren't able to frame their world with the Word, because they don't know what the Word says.

Now let's look at the last part of that verse in Matthew 11:29: **For I am meek and lowly in heart: and ye shall find rest unto your souls.** How do you learn of Jesus' lowliness in heart? Through spending time with Him and His Word. If you fail to learn of Jesus through the Word, even though you have "come to Him," you will never find His rest. You may be born again, but your mind will not be clear. It won't be full of rest and peace, because it's burdened down with cares.

Jesus' yoke is easy and His burden is light. When you are in true fellowship with Him and His yoke is upon you, you should not feel heavy hearted and your mind should not be burdened. First Peter 5:7 (AMP) says,

> **Casting the whole of your care—all your anxieties, all your worries, all your concerns, once and for all—on Him; for He cares for you affectionately, and cares about you watchfully.**

Notice it says, "Casting the whole of your care." That means, in essence, *casting every part of whatever care it is you have.* Then it also gives examples of what cares entail: anxieties, worries and concerns.

Then it says to do it *once and for all.* In other words, you don't give your cares to the Lord for a certain period of time and then take them back. No, you give them to Him one time, and you never take them back.

"Why should I cast all my care on the Lord?" someone might ask. Because the Lord loves His children. Because He cares for us. How does He care for us? *Affectionately and watchfully.*

The Lord is watching over us, and He is saying to us, "Give those cares to Me. I can handle them. I am the Lord."

Think about some of the things you may be dealing with right now, whether it is a situation concerning your spouse, sickness, lack of finances, trouble on your job, uncertainty concerning the future, a broken relationship with a friend or family member or something that has caused you anxiety, worry or concern. As you are thinking of the specific things that you've been carrying, I want you to name them out loud one by one and say from your heart, "Lord, I'm casting this upon You."

When you do that, you're not throwing away the care. You're casting it away from you, but you're casting it *on the Lord.* You're saying to Him, "Lord, I'm trusting You. I give this care to You, and I refuse to worry about it anymore. I won't touch the matter again in my thought life, because I know You've got it now. It's not mine to carry anymore. If I do think of it again, I'm going to praise You for what You're doing about it. As far as I'm concerned, it's settled."

God doesn't want you to worry about a thing. Why? Because worry will keep you from having the mind of Christ. It will keep you from being able to frame your world with His Word. God is well able to handle your problems. If you could have solved them yourself, you would have already done it. So give them to Him. But He won't take them if you're holding on to them. You have to cast them on Him. He cares for you, and He will take care of you.

Learn to cast down evil imaginations, and don't be afraid to deal authoritatively with the devil if you need to. Cast him out of your life. He is not your master; *Jesus* is your Master. And Jesus gave you His name to deal with any devil or demon that would try to hinder you.

Also, make sure you cast every care on the Lord. You have to free yourself so you can think God's thoughts. Now you're ready to frame your world!

5

Faith Is of the Heart

n review, "A" is *right thinking,* "B" is *right believing* and "C" is *right speaking* or *right confessing.* We must learn these three in order because we have to *think* right to *believe* right, and we have to believe right to *confess* right.

Thinking has to do with the mind. Believing has to do with the heart or spirit. And speaking or confessing has to do with the mouth. These three areas—thinking, believing and speaking—deal with the total man and, if governed properly, will set him up to receive multiplied blessings.

The person who aligns his thinking, his believing and his speaking with the Word will be in cooperation with God in bringing him from sickness into health, from poverty into wealth, from bondage into complete liberty, from a life of gloom into great joy and from confusion into utter peace.

In this chapter, we are going to be dealing with the "B" part of the ABC's of framing your world: believing.

Believing is connected with the heart. Romans 10:10 says, **For with the heart man believeth unto righteousness; and with the mouth confession is made unto salvation.**

Remember I said that you *are* a spirit, you *have* a soul and you *live in* a body. (1 Thess. 5:23.) If you don't know this fact, the devil will play tricks on you with situations, circumstances and feelings—things that have to do with the sense realm.

You are a spiritual being, and in the new birth, your spirit was born again. However, you still have the same mind and the same body you had before you were born again. When you understand that your mind and body weren't born again in the new birth, then when feelings come that are contrary to God's Word, you can reach down into the inner resource of your spirit and dominate your mind and your body. If you maintain your spirit properly, feeding and strengthening your inner man with the Word, you can overcome what your flesh is saying to you.

Proverbs 3:5 says, **Trust in the Lord with all thine heart** [or spirit]; **and lean not unto thine own understanding** [or mind]. This verse further illustrates the fact that your heart and mind are not the same. Remember I said you could have faith in your heart while you're having doubt in your head. That's why this verse says, "Trust the Lord with your heart and lean not unto your mind."

So we know that your heart and your mind are not the same. Your heart (or spirit) and your body are not the same either. Let's look at a familiar verse in Romans 12:1 to illustrate that fact:

> I beseech you therefore, brethren, by the mercies of God, that ye present your bodies a living sacrifice, holy, acceptable unto God, which is your reasonable service.

When Paul talks about "ye" in this verse, he is talking about the real you, your spirit. Your spirit, the real you, is supposed to present your body, your temporary "earth suit," as a living sacrifice to God.

Let's look at another familiar verse. First Corinthians 9:27 says, **But I keep under my body, and bring it into subjection: lest that by any means, when I have preached to others, I myself should be a castaway.**

Who is the "I" referring to in this verse? It can't be referring to Paul's body, because then it would read, "My body keeps my body under." No, "I" in this verse is talking about the real Paul, Paul's spirit. So we know that the spirit and body are not the same.

As I said, you *are* a spirit, you *have* a soul and you *live in* a body. When the Bible talks about the heart of man, it's talking about the spirit of man. The heart is also referred to in the Bible as the inner man or the hidden man of the heart.

There was a time in my Christian walk when, although I was living right and holy, I struggled to walk closely with God. I would say, "Lord, just give me more faith. I want to walk with You." But then I found out how to operate out of my spirit, and it changed my life.

Hebrews 11:6 says, **But without faith it is impossible to please him.** To walk closely with God, you have to know something about faith. But you can't walk by faith with your mind or your body. You walk by faith with your *heart,* because faith is of the heart.

The Key to Victory

We read Proverbs 3:5, which says, **Trust in the Lord with all thine heart; and lean not unto thine own understanding** [mind]. This verse is the key to victory. You've probably heard it said, and it's true: If Satan can keep you in the arena of reason—in other words, in the arena of the mind—he will whip you every time. But if you can hold him in the arena of faith—in the arena of believing with the heart—you will defeat him in every combat. *One of the greatest secrets to faith you can learn is that faith is of the heart.* It's not of the mind, and it's not of the body.

Man, whether he is with or without God, is an eternal being. When he dies, his spirit lives on—either with God in heaven or without God in hell.

Eternity is in your spirit. If you come into right relationship with God, you'll have eternal life. If you *don't* come into relationship with God, you'll have eternal damnation.

So we know that man is a spiritual being. And whether it be salvation, the baptism in the Holy Spirit, healing, finances or some other blessing, you receive these things by faith or by believing with the spirit or heart. That's His plan; that's the way He set it up. And your heart has to be involved with it because faith is of the heart.

Your Flesh Will Resist Believing God

Think about the ways the church has been trying to receive from God. We've tried everything but believing. We've tried doing good works, bargaining with God, having positive mental energy and trying to make something happen in ourselves, in our own strength. But we have resisted believing God.

According to the Bible, unbelief is a serious thing with God. Looking at Old Testament examples, we don't find accounts of God smiling on unbelief.

There are two types of unbelief. The first kind is unbelief which is caused by ignorance. In other words, people doubt because they don't know the truth. The other kind of unbelief is the serious kind. It's unbelief caused by people who know the truth but who can't be persuaded to believe or act on the Word of God. The cure for the first kind of unbelief is to study the Word of God. The cure for the second kind of unbelief is obedience to the Word.

All the answers you need from God can be yours if you will take His Word and obey it, believing it with your heart independently of circumstances and independently of what your mind or body is telling you.

Romans 10:10 says, **With the heart man believeth....** Well, since you're supposed to believe God with your heart independently of your mind and body, that must mean you can separate your spirit, soul and body. First Thessalonians 5:23 says,

> **And the very God of peace sanctify you wholly; and I pray God your whole spirit and soul and body be preserved blameless unto the coming of our Lord Jesus Christ.**

There is a separation here, and you see all three listed separately. So I believe this verse further establishes that the heart, the mind and the body are separate. They're not the same.

Hebrews 4:12 states,

> **For the word of God is quick, and powerful, and sharper than any two edged sword, piercing even to the dividing asunder of soul and spirit, and of the joints and marrow, and is a discerner of the thoughts and intents of the heart.**

This verse is talking about the dividing of soul and spirit. Well, if the soul and the spirit of man were the same, they wouldn't have to be divided. Faith is of the heart or spirit. It's not of the head or of the soul, which consists of the mind and emotions.

Heart Faith Believes God Despite the Circumstances

Have you ever heard the expression "head faith"? A person who's operating in head faith is trying to believe God with his mind. He mentally assents that the Word of God is true, but that's where he stops. When the time comes to act on the Word, his head won't let him do it. His mind can only go so far, because the mind needs some feeling to go along with its believing. The mind can't believe God independently of or apart from circumstances.

But when you really have the Word of God deposited into your spirit, you'll act on it no matter what the circumstances, and you'll keep acting on it even if you don't see anything happening. Why? Because you believe it in your heart. You don't have to see, hear or feel the answer. You *believe*. Faith is of the heart.

You Are To Rule and Reign in Life

In my many years of ministry, I have seen children of God just thrown from one side of the highway to the other, so to speak. But you don't have any business being tossed from one side of the highway to the other. You *are* the highway! In other words, you're calling the shots, not Satan and not the circumstances. I mean, you should be putting out stop signs and detour signs when *you* get ready!

Romans 5:17 says,

> **For if by one man's** [Adam's] **offence death reigned by one; much more they which receive abundance of grace and of the gift of righteousness shall reign in life by one, Jesus Christ.**

You should rule and reign over circumstances instead of letting circumstances rule and reign over you. But you have to do it out of your spirit. The Word of God has to be in your heart, because faith cometh by hearing, and hearing by the Word of God (Rom. 10:17), and faith is of the heart.

Jesus, in dealing with the Pharisee Nicodemus, said, **That which is born of the flesh is flesh; and that which is born of the Spirit is spirit** (John 3:6). If we're trying to deal with God out of our heads or out of our feelings, then what we're doing is trying to deal with God out of our flesh. But God is a Spirit. And according to John 4:24 there is only one way to connect with God; **God is a Spirit: and they that worship him must worship him in spirit and in truth.**

Your Spirit Must Be Trained and Developed

It takes time to develop your spirit. You're not going to hear one message or read one verse of Scripture and immediately have your heart filled with faith. No, you have to walk it out. There are stages of development. You have to train your re-created human spirit with the Word so that yielding to your spirit with your mouth—with what you say— is easy.

So many times we want to yield our tongue to our head—to what we see, hear or feel, or to our thoughts because it's easier. The flesh does not like to walk by faith. It likes to walk by sight or by the senses. As we just read, Jesus said, **That which is born of the flesh is flesh; and that which is born of the Spirit is spirit** (John 3:6).

Let's look in more detail at the spirit of man. John 7:37-39 says:

In the last day, that great day of the feast, Jesus stood and cried, saying, If any man thirst, let him come unto me, and drink.

He that believeth on me, as the scripture hath said, out of his belly shall flow rivers of living water.

(But this spake he of the Spirit, which they that believe on him should receive: for the Holy Ghost was not yet given; because that Jesus was not yet glorified.)

What is the word *belly* referring to in this verse? It's referring to the spirit of man. What are the "rivers of living waters"? They are the Holy Spirit.

You see, God communicates with man Spirit to spirit. In other words, if you're born again, the Holy Spirit speaks to your spirit. For example, Romans 8:16 says, **The Spirit itself** [or Himself] **beareth witness with our spirit, that we are the children of God.**

First Corinthians 14:14 says, **For if I pray in an unknown tongue, my spirit prayeth, but my understanding** [or mind] **is unfruitful.** You see, those unknown tongues are coming out of my spirit, not my mind. My spirit is a line to God. I'm praying secrets that only my Father knows. My understanding doesn't know, unless it is revealed to my mind by the Holy Spirit. And the devil doesn't know those divine secrets either. So your inner man communes with the Father. Your spirit is in connection with God, who is a Spirit.

Your Spirit Can Bypass Your Mind

Paul said, **"My understanding is unfruitful."** He meant that his understanding—his natural, mental understanding, or his mind—was unfruitful when he was praying in the Spirit. He was speaking mysteries unto God in other tongues.

That's why so many people do not operate in the Spirit. Their understanding is unfruitful, and they want to understand everything about it before they have anything to do with it.

Sometimes when the Holy Spirit moves in my ministry, I just follow Him and obey His instructions by faith. My mind doesn't know what's going to happen next. I'm walking totally by faith. My mind is screaming, *Oh, no, don't do that! What if it doesn't work? What will everyone think?* But by ignoring and bypassing the questions in my mind and stepping out in the Spirit, I've seen countless people healed, delivered and set completely free.

Now don't misunderstand me. I'm not saying you're not supposed to think or use your mind. God gave you a mind and you're to use it. For example, you need your understanding to know when to cross the street in traffic!

But right now, I'm talking about heavenly things. The natural mind doesn't always understand them, so you have to bypass your mind. You can't hold on to your senses and move with God, who is a Spirit. You can't hold on to what you can feel, touch, taste and so forth. You have to trust God and have faith in Him. And, remember, faith is of the heart.

Paul said when he prayed in the Spirit, his understanding was unfruitful. You know, your understanding is what brings fear, doubt and unbelief. Your understanding is the thing that gets you into problems while you're trying to figure everything out yourself. That's compromise, and anything you compromise to keep, you'll lose. You simply can't operate by feelings and walk by faith at the same time. It won't work.

Someone might ask, "Yes, but isn't denying your feelings a form of brainwashing?" I'm not talking about denying your feelings as much as I'm talking about not allowing your feelings to come between you and God!

If God said it, I believe it and that settles it for me. Even if my feelings tell me something different, I'm staying with the Word. I'm going to stick with operating out of my heart rather than out of my head.

Now let's look at the next verse in 1 Corinthians 14:15:

> **What is it then? I will pray with the spirit, and I will pray with the understanding also: I will sing with the spirit, and I will sing with the understanding also.**

Feelings, which are a part of the mind, are unreliable. They are uncertain, unsteady and unstable. They can't be depended on. But when your understanding gets connected with your spirit, you can depend on your understanding. So how do you keep your understanding connected with your spirit? One way is by speaking the Word only. John 6:63 says, **It is the spirit that quickeneth; the** flesh profiteth nothing: the words that I speak unto you, they are spirit, and they are life. God's Word is Spirit and life.

Let's look at one more verse that distinguishes the heart (the spirit) from the flesh (the soul, or the mind and emotions). Second Corinthians 4:16 says, For which cause we faint not; but though our outward man perish, yet the inward man is renewed day by day. In this portion of Scripture, Paul is talking about two men—the outward man and the inward man. One is dying, and the other is coming alive more and more.

Whether we know it or not or even believe it or not, we are dying. Our outward man is perishing little by little. The Bible says so. You can know your rights in Christ, but your outward man is still decaying. But you can use your inward man to make the outward man live longer. I can prove it by the Bible. Romans 8:11 says,

> But if the Spirit of him that raised up Jesus from the dead dwell in you, he that raised up Christ from the dead shall also quicken your mortal bodies by his Spirit that dwelleth in you.

Where does that verse say the Holy Spirit—the Spirit of Him who raised Jesus from the dead—dwells? What does "quicken" mean? It means *to make alive*. You see, your inward man—the Holy Spirit in your spirit—can quicken your outward man, your mortal body.

Let the Word of God in Your Spirit Dominate Your Body

If you loose the Spirit of God in your re-created spirit and begin to live out of your spirit, your body will line up. I know my body did. I used to cry every week about how sick I was. The devil once tried to put nine colds on me in a period of two weeks! He was trying, but he was lying! I knew what the Word said, and I had that Word in my heart. If I had been going by feelings alone, I would have jumped into bed sick. But I let that spirit man on the inside rise up. I let the Word of God dominate my thoughts and my feelings, or what my body was telling me about how sick I was.

When the devil came against me with symptoms, I said from my heart, "Oh, no you don't! I don't accept colds; I don't accept the flu! I submit myself to God. Therefore, I can resist this."

Let your spirit man rise up and let your tongue speak in line with your heart, with your believing. The way you loose the Spirit of God into your life is through your words, through your right speaking. You can say, "By Jesus' stripes I *was* healed, and I *am* healed. Christ has redeemed me from the curse of the Law. I'm the redeemed of the Lord."

Learn to live out of your spirit in every area of your life. You even need to live out of your spirit when you're learning about spiritual things. First John 2:20 says, **But ye have an unction** [an anointing] **from the Holy One, and ye know all things.** Where is that unction? It's in your spirit.

Verse 27 says,

> But the anointing which ye have received of him abideth in you [in your spirit], and ye need not that any man teach you: but as the same anointing teacheth you of all things, and is truth, and is no lie, and even as it hath taught you, ye shall abide in him.

You need to have the anointing of God to receive anointed teaching! You can't go to church without praying and simply sit there in the pew, waiting, and expect to receive something! You can't go with a haphazard, I-don't-care attitude. You have to have your spiritual antenna up. You have to be living out of your spirit.

Hebrews 11:3 says,

> Through faith we understand that the worlds were framed by the word of God, so that things which are seen were not made of things which do appear.

You see, if you don't have any faith, you're not going to have any spiritual understanding.

For example, when you know that most women can no longer naturally conceive children after the age of about fifty, give or take a few years, you simply can't understand out of your head how a ninety-year-old woman can have a baby, as in the case of Abraham's wife, Sarah. But by faith you can understand it. They had Isaac according to what God had spoken. God had told them that they were going to have a child who was going to be their heir. (Gen. 15.)

And, believe me, Abraham had to walk that whole scenario out by faith. He had to dominate his natural thinking with his spirit and give first place to what he believed based on what God's Word, not on the circumstances.

And Abraham successfully lived out of his spirit, for Romans 4:18-21 says about Abraham: (1) He *against hope believed in hope*; (2) he *considered not his own body now dead*, and, therefore, *was not weak in faith*, but, instead, *gave glory to God*; (3) he *staggered not at the promise of God through unbelief*; but *was strong in faith, giving glory to God*; and (4) he *was fully persuaded that, what God had promised, He was able also to perform.*

We ought to walk in faith as Abraham walked. Abraham brought his mind and body under subjection. The apostle Paul said that we have to bring our bodies under subjection by living out of our spirits (1 Cor. 9:27). In other words, we are not to cry to God, saying, "Lord, keep me from doing this thing, or keep me from doing that thing." No, out of our spirits, *we* are each to keep our bodies under and keep them from trying to have their own way.

If you walk only by your senses, Satan is going to see to it that you are sick, broke, confused and oppressed. And if you don't know how to shut him down and cast him out, he'll eventually take control of your life. So learn to walk in the Spirit and keep yourself in the arena of faith, where you will emerge the victor in combat. With your thinking straight and your believing

6

The Secret of Faith

ome people want to argue the point that it's good to have a positive confession, but that your thinking and believing have nothing to do with your confession. They say that what you think is really not important as long as you have a positive confession.

But I can prove to you by the Word that if your thinking is not right and your believing is not right, then your mouth is not going to consistently say the right thing. Even if you make a positive confession every once in a while, no power from heaven will be produced if your thinking and believing are wrong.

> **O generation of vipers, how can ye, being evil, speak good things? for out of the abundance of the heart the mouth speaketh. A good man out of the good treasure of the heart bringeth forth good things: and an evil man out of the evil treasure bringeth forth evil things.**
>
> **Matthew 12:34,35**

You know, Jesus could be hard at times. For instance, here He called the Pharisees a bunch of snakes! Then in that same verse He said, **How can ye, being evil, speak good things?** He was saying, "How can you, having an evil mind and an evil heart, speak anything good?"

Now I want you to read verse 35 again and pay close attention to what it says: **A good man out of the good treasure of the heart bringeth forth good things: and an evil man out of the evil treasure bringeth forth evil things.**

The first phrase is, "A good man." Every child of God is good. When I say "good," I mean he or she has the nature of God inside. Now a person may not be *acting* like he's good, and others may not *see* him as good, but he *is* good because he has the life of God in him.

What is the "good treasure of the heart?" Well, let's say, for example, that your heart is a bank. You make deposits into that bank by what you think, believe and say. So the good treasure of the heart could be the Word of God, because the Word most certainly is a good treasure.

I always encourage people to read, study and meditate constantly on God's Word. But, even if you do that, it's hard to keep good treasure in your heart if you're going to a church where the Word isn't taught. You should attend a church where you can be fed spiritually, where you can hear the Word of God preached.

When the Word of God is constantly before you—through personal study, hearing good sermons, listening to good teaching tapes and so forth—deposits are being made into you from which you can draw when you need them.

A good treasure in this verse is talking about a good deposit. What are you depositing into *your* heart?

When God Has a Pattern, He Always Has a Plan

I said in a previous chapter that to frame your world means to fashion it according to God's pattern, according to the mind of Christ. We know that God's pattern is love, peace, joy, health, life and material prosperity.

Now let's look back at Matthew 12:34,35:

Out of the abundance of the heart the mouth speaketh. A good man out of the good treasure of the heart bringeth forth good things.

It says that a good man out of the good treasure of his heart brings forth good things. The good treasure is the Word. So from the Word of God which is deposited in a person's heart, he brings forth good things. Exactly how does he bring forth those good things? With his mouth! Out of the abundance of your heart your mouth speaks!

So I submit to you that since Jesus said, "Out of the good treasure of his heart, a good man brings forth good things," He has given us a plan as to *how* to bring them forth.

Spiritual Deposits and Withdrawals

As I said, your heart, or your spirit, is like a bank. Whatever you put into your heart is your deposit. Well, your withdrawals are made with your mouth, by your making the proper confession based on the Word that's in your heart.

By way of illustration, if you had no debt and you had $100,000 in the bank, you wouldn't go to the bank and say, "I owe you $100,000, and I need to pay it." No, if you did that, the teller would think you were out of our mind! He might not even let you make a withdrawal, or a demand on your account, if you were talking like that. Why? Because you're saying the wrong thing.

But if you said to that teller, "I want my $100,000," he or she would give it to you, because that money is yours; it belongs to you. By your saying, "Please give me my $100,000," you would be exercising your rights as an account holder who possesses $100,000.

So out of the good treasure of the heart, a person brings forth good things. And the *way* he brings forth those good things is with his mouth. You see, when your heart is full of the good treasure of the Word, you can speak that Word out and bring forth good things in your life, whether it be healing, deliverance or some other blessing you have need of.

In other words, the deposits you have made into your heart can be loosed out of your mouth by faith. When that happens, in the spirit world, God the Father, Jesus, the Holy Ghost and God's angels all go to work to make sure that what you're speaking comes to pass for you. If what you're speaking is faith in the Word, God will cause good things to be brought forth in your life.

A good man out of the good treasure of the heart bringeth forth good things. Good brings forth good! A good treasure in your heart can bring forth good things for you. Your circumstances may look bad, but if you have a good treasure in your heart, good can come forth.

Learn To Think and Talk About the Invisible

We have been so trained mentally, which isn't wrong in itself, that we sometimes forget we need to think spiritually too. We need to think about the supernatural and the invisible. Remember our main text in Hebrews 11:3 said, **Through faith we understand that the worlds were framed by the word of God, so that things which are seen were not made of things which do appear.** In other words, things which are seen were made of things which do *not* appear, or which are invisible.

So we need to think, believe and speak, not according to things which are seen—our circumstances—but according to things which are not seen—the Word of God. As we are faithful to think, believe and speak according to that which is not seen, God will make those things tangible in our lives. He will make them "seen!"

> **A good man out of the good treasure of the heart bringeth forth good things: and an evil man out of the evil treasure bringeth forth evil things.**   Matthew 12:35

I once heard someone say, "I'm born again, but I don't feel like a good man." Well, if you are born again, you don't have to try to figure out whether or not you're a good man. Your goodness is not of yourself; it's of God. You are good because you have the Good One in you! What you need to do now is hook up with what you have and what you are in Christ. Find out what belongs to you; then think on and believe *it*. Next, make the proper connection by speaking it out, and the "good things" are going to come forth.

So we don't have to discuss who is good and who is not good. If you're born again, you're good. If you're not born again, you can become good by accepting Jesus Christ as your Savior.

'Ask What Ye Will'

Let's look at another Scripture in connection with that thought. In John 15:7, Jesus said, **If ye abide in me, and my words abide in you, ye shall ask what ye will, and it shall be done unto you.** *It's the same as Jesus' saying,* "You're a good man. You're a good woman. My Word is good treasure and it brings forth good things. So put it into your heart and ask God what you will!"

The Negative Side of the Truth

I said that your words can set you free or they can imprison you. There is a positive and a negative side to Matthew 12:35 because the Bible deals with both the positive and negative sides of things. First, the Lord points to the positive. He says, **A good man**

out the good treasure of the heart bringeth forth good things.
In other words, He might say, "My child, this is what belongs to
you. Fill your heart with My Word, and good things will come
forth."

Then, the Lord talks about the negative: **An evil man out of
the evil treasure bringeth forth evil things.** He could also say it
another way: "This is what happens to the wicked person who
doesn't obey My Word."

Off With the Old and On With the New

Your faith can do a lot of things. Jesus said it could move
mountains. (Mark 11:23.) Well, if your faith can move mountains, it
can certainly help you receive healing for your body, peace for your
home and money for the things you need and want.

But, as I said before, there are often a lot of things we have to
*un*do in our lives before our faith begins to work to such a degree
that we can see the results it's producing in our lives. For example,
if you had your car painted the wrong color and you took it back
to have it repainted, the person who painted your car in the first
place is not simply going to put another coat of paint on your car.
No, first he's going to have to remove, or scrape off the old paint.

Similarly, before you "paint" your life the color you want it to
be, or before you frame your world the way you want to have it
framed, you're probably going to have to scrape off some the old

ways of thinking, believing and speaking that have gotten you into the position you're in today.

It doesn't happen overnight either; it takes time. But the same way you frame your world—with right thinking, right believing and right speaking—is the same way you *un*frame the things in your life that need to be unframed. You think the right things, you believe the right things and you speak the right things, and eventually the old things are scraped away and replaced with the new. The secret is having a heart that is yielded to God's Word and making a good confession.

7

'And God Said...'

Through faith we understand that
the worlds were framed by the word of
God, so that things which are seen were
not made of things which do appear.

HEBREWS 11:3

This whole universe—the sun, the moon, the stars, the planets and everything else contained in it—was framed by God. How does it say He framed the worlds? *By His Word.* God framed the worlds with His Word.

We know that in framing the worlds with His Word, God not only created the universe, but in so doing, He also laid down a pattern for us to follow. We can speak things into existence in our own lives with His Word and we can frame our world with the Word of God.

Let's look at the story of creation in Genesis 1.

In the beginning God created the heaven and the earth. And the earth was without form, and void; and darkness was upon the face of the deep. And the Spirit of God moved upon the face of the waters. And God said, Let there be light: and there was light.

...And God said, Let there be a firmament in the midst of the waters, and let it divide the waters from the waters. And God made the firmament, and divided the waters which were under the firmament from the waters which were above the firmament: and it was so.

...And God said, Let the waters under the heaven be gathered together unto one place, and let the dry land appear: and it was so... And God said, Let the earth bring forth grass, the herb yielding seed, and the fruit tree yielding fruit after his kind, whose seed is in itself, upon the earth: and it was so.

...And God said, Let there be lights in the firmament of the heaven to divide the day from the night; and let them be for signs, and for seasons, and for days, and years: and let them be for lights in the firmament of the heaven to give light upon the earth: and it was so.

...And God said, Let the waters bring forth abundantly the moving creature that hath life, and fowl that may fly above the earth in the open firmament of heaven. And God created great whales, and every living creature that moveth, which the waters brought forth abundantly, after their kind, and every winged fowl after his kind: and God saw that it was good.

> And God said, Let the earth bring forth the living creature
> after his kind, cattle, and creeping thing, and beast of the earth
> after his kind: and it was so.
>
> Genesis 1:1-3,6,7,9,11,14,15,20,21,24

It's amazing how God kept saying the same thing over and over again—"And God said."

One could ask the question, "Why did God feel He had to do that? It seems Genesis 1 could have simply read, "And God said, 'Let there be light, a firmament, waters, grass...'" and so forth. Instead, it says over and over again, "And God said...." There was a reason.

Genesis 1 was written this way for a reason. God was emphasizing His authority, laying down a pattern and showing us His *modus operandi*, His "MO" or His way of operating and getting things done. God is a faith God, and He speaks forth faith words. As children of a faith God, we are to speak faith words too.

Jesus—The Will of the Father in Action

Really, all we have to do is follow after Jesus, because Jesus said, "He who has seen Me has seen the Father. Whatever I see My Father do, that I do." (John 6:46; 8:28; 10:30; 14:9.) Jesus acted just like His Daddy! Jesus was present with God the Father when God said in the beginning, "Let there be...." So when Jesus came on the scene, He already understood this principle. And He showed us what to do in the story of the fig tree.

And on the morrow, when they were come from Bethany, he [Jesus] was hungry: and seeing a fig tree afar off having leaves, he came, if haply he might find anything thereon: and when he came to it, he found nothing but leaves; for the time of figs was not yet.

And Jesus answered and said unto it, No man eat fruit of thee hereafter for ever. And his disciples heard it.

And when even was come, he went out of the city. And in the morning, as they passed by, they saw the fig tree dried up from the roots. And Peter calling to remembrance saith unto him, Master, behold, the fig tree which thou cursedst is withered away.

And Jesus answering saith unto them, Have faith in God [Or, "Have the faith *of* God"].

Mark 11:12-14,19-22

The disciples saw firsthand how Jesus followed God's pattern for framing worlds. In Mark 11:14, it says, **And Jesus said unto it** [the fig tree]**, No man eat fruit of thee hereafter for ever.** Now look at verse 20: **And in the morning, as they passed by, they saw the fig tree dried up from the roots.** In other words, Jesus said it, and it was so!

Jesus was following God's pattern, as we are to follow God's pattern. Remember we read this verse in Ephesians 5:1: **Be ye therefore followers of God as dear children.** Therefore, we can do the same thing God and Jesus did. We can bring things into existence with God's Word. We can speak to mountains—

hindrances in our lives—and tell them to move. Your mind may be baffled by this fact, just as I'm sure the disciples' minds were baffled when they heard Jesus talking to that fig tree.

The disciples were human just like we are. They probably thought Jesus was losing it when they heard Him talking to that tree! I'm sure they'd never heard anyone talk to a tree before. Some of them might have thought, *Hey, I don't know if I should go any further with this dude or not!*

I'm sure the disciples were wondering what they'd gotten themselves into by following Jesus. In the same way, you may wonder and question what you're doing when you speak to your mountains. I'm sure the devil probably said to the disciples, "Look at you! You're following a guy who talks to trees!" But, you see, the lesson was being taught. Jesus was teaching the disciples how to frame their world with the Word.

Now let's go back to verse 20 to learn an important key to framing your world. It says, **And in the morning, as they passed by, they saw the fig tree dried up from the roots.**

Jesus had cursed that tree at least one day prior to this time. In other words, nothing happened instantly when Jesus spoke to the tree. Here is the lesson: When you speak to something on Wednesday, the situation might not be resolved by Friday. That's why it's important to hold fast to your confession without wavering. (Heb. 10:23.)

The fig tree didn't dry up the moment Jesus spoke to it. But as far as Jesus was concerned, it was a dead tree as soon as He spoke the words. What caused the fig tree in Mark 11 to finally dry up? *Words.* Jesus had seen His Father talk to water and tell it to come into existence. Jesus knew how to use words.

And Peter calling to remembrance saith unto him, Master, behold, the fig tree which thou cursedst is withered away.

Mark 11:21

Peter was excited. He said, "Master, it happened just like You said it would!"

Jesus said to Peter and the other disciples, "You can do the same thing." Mark 11:22 says, **And Jesus answering saith unto them** [the disciples], **Have faith in God.**

Jesus was saying, "The thing that caused this tree to die was My Daddy's kind of faith." Then Jesus said, "Now I'm going to show you how it works."

For verily I say unto you, That whosoever shall say unto this mountain, Be thou removed, and be thou cast into the sea; and shall not doubt in his heart, but shall believe that those things which he saith shall come to pass; he shall have whatsoever he saith.

Mark 11:23

Jesus was talking about believing and speaking. He was talking about making a Word-based confession. He wasn't talking about prayer, but He did cover prayer in the very next verse.

> Therefore I say unto you, What things soever ye desire,
> when ye pray, believe that ye receive them, and ye shall have
> them.
>
> Mark 11:24

Jesus was saying that prayer works in the same way—*praying* works the same way as *saying*. Jesus said, "When you pray [and when you pray, you're saying something], believe in your heart that you receive whatever it is you're praying for, and you will have it."

You can pray the prayer of faith for yourself and get an answer from God every time. But you have to know how faith operates. You have to believe something independently of circumstances or independently of what you can or cannot see. According to Mark 11:24, you have to believe you receive the answer, not when you have it in your hand, but *the minute that you pray!* It says, *When ye pray, believe that ye receive them, and ye shall have them.*

When Jesus cursed the fig tree, it was dead the minute He spoke the words. However, the manifestation of it wasn't apparent until the next day.

Let that sink in. You believe you receive when you pray. Then the manifestation of whatever it is you prayed for is God's job. You just hold fast to your confession of faith, because God is faithful.

Let's look at some biblical examples of people who followed God's pattern and framed their world with the Word of God.

The Woman With the Issue of Blood

The woman with the issue of blood is an example of someone who held fast to her confession of faith without wavering, and she received a great deliverance.

And a certain woman, which had an issue of blood twelve years,

And had suffered many things of many physicians, and had spent all that she had, and was nothing bettered, but rather grew worse,

When she had heard of Jesus, came in the press behind, and touched his garment.

For she said, If I may touch but his clothes, I shall be whole.

And straightway the fountain of her blood was dried up; and she felt in her body that she was healed of that plague.

And Jesus, immediately knowing in himself that virtue had gone out of him, turned him about in the press, and said, Who touched my clothes?

And his disciples said unto him, Thou seest the multitude thronging thee, and sayest thou, Who touched me?

And he looked round about to see her that had done this thing.

But the woman fearing and trembling, knowing what was done in her, came and fell down before him, and told him all the truth.

**And he said unto her, Daughter, thy faith hath made thee
whole; go in peace, and be whole of thy plague.**

Mark 5:25-34

It says about this woman that she'd had an issue of blood for
twelve years, that she had suffered many things of many physicians,
that she had spent everything she had, and that she was nothing
better. In fact, she grew worse.

But this woman was getting ready to enter another realm—the
realm of faith! Verse 27 says, **....when she had heard of Jesus....**
Remember we said that "faith cometh by hearing, and hearing by
the Word of God." (Rom. 10:17.)

When faith came to her, the woman *said* something very important. **She said, If I may touch but his clothes, I shall be whole.**

What did the woman say? She said, **...If I may touch but his
clothes, I shall be whole.** Notice that she *didn't* confess her
sickness, her doctors' failures, her suffering and her lack. She'd
stopped talking about all of that. Instead, she began to say what
she'd heard about Jesus.

Now look at verse 34 again: **And he said unto her, Daughter,
thy faith hath made thee whole; go in peace, and be whole of
thy plague.** Whose faith made the woman whole? Was it Jesus'
faith? No, it was *her* faith. The woman got her thinking, believing
and confessing straight after she'd heard of Jesus. She quit talking
about suffering and dying, and she began to talk about living well

and whole. She said, "Hey, that Man I heard about—if I can get to Him, I'm going to be all right. I'm going to be whole again!"

When the woman touched Jesus' garment and power went out of Him, He said, ...**Who touched my clothes?** You see, Jesus knew immediately when the power went out of Him, but He didn't know who had touched Him. That must mean that the power was present to heal any one of those people in that crowd. But only one person, the woman with the issue of blood, made a demand on that power. James 1:22 says, **Be ye doers of the word, and not hearers only, deceiving your own selves.**

What would have happened if the woman with the issue of blood had said, "If I but touch the hem of His garment, I shall be whole," but then she didn't act on it or do anything about it? Nothing would have happened!

You have to make your confession. You have to find out what the Word says and start saying that. But then you have to act on what you believe and what you say. The woman with the issue of blood said, "If I may touch but His clothes, I'll be well." But then she set out to actually touch Jesus' clothes. She was a doer of the Word and not a hearer only. She heard, she believed, she said and then she did. And Jesus told her that it was her faith which had made her whole.

David and Goliath

David was just a shepherd boy when he began framing his world with the Word of God. First Samuel 17 gives the account of Goliath, the mighty Philistine who taunted Israel's armies day and night for forty days. Some say that Goliath was more than nine feet tall and had been a warrior from his youth. He said to Israel, "Send a man over to fight with me. If he wins, we will serve you. But if I win, you will serve us" (vv. 8,9).

Now the Israelite army was **...dismayed, and greatly afraid** (v. 11). Three of David's older brothers were in that army, but David had stayed home to tend his father's sheep. David was visiting his brothers with provisions sent from their father when he found himself right in the middle of all the commotion.

When David heard that the king would give great riches and honor to the man who killed Goliath, he asked,

> **What shall be done to the man that killeth this Philistine, and taketh away the reproach from Israel? for who is this uncircumcised Philistine, that he should defy the armies of the living God?**
>
> 1 Samuel 17:26

David was framing his world with words!

David finally asked so many questions that word got to King Saul, and the king sent for David. David then said to Saul, **Let no man's heart fail because of him; thy servant will go and fight with this Philistine** (v. 32).

Saul argued with David at first, saying that David was just a boy and certainly was not able to take on Goliath. But then David began to rehearse the victories God had given him in the past.

And David said unto Saul, Thy servant kept his father's sheep, and there came a lion, and a bear, and took a lamb out of the flock:

And I went out after him, and smote him, and delivered it out of his mouth: and when he arose against me, I caught him by his beard, and smote him, and slew him.

Thy servant slew both the lion and the bear: and this uncircumcised Philistine shall be as one of them, seeing he hath defied the armies of the living God.

David said moreover, The Lord that delivered me out of the paw of the lion, and out of the paw of the bear, he will deliver me out of the hand of this Philistine....

1 Samuel 17:34-37

When Saul heard all that, he said to David, ...Go, and the Lord be with thee (v. 37). In other words, Saul said, "I'm not going with you. You go, and the Lord be with you!"

And Saul armed David with his armour, and he put an helmet of brass upon his head; also he armed him with a coat of mail.

And David girded his sword upon his armour, and he assayed to go; for he had not proved it. And David said unto Saul, I cannot go with these; for I have not proved them. And David put them off him.   1 Samuel 17:38,39

David was saying, "I can't use these things; I haven't proved them."

How many times in spiritual battle do we try to use everything we can get our hands on—except the Word of God? We try to find answers in our own strength. We try to solicit help from others or try to work it out ourselves. It seems we're afraid to trust the Word of God, and it's the greatest weapon we could ever have.

David wasn't afraid to use spiritual weapons because he had been proving them as a shepherd boy while taking care of his father's sheep. He knew that God had helped him slay the lion and the bear, and he knew that God was going to help him slay Goliath too.

And he took his staff in his hand, and chose him five smooth stones out of the brook, and put them in a shepherd's bag which he had, even in a scrip; and his sling was in his hand: and he drew near to the Philistine.

1 Samuel 17:40

Now let's see how David held on to his confession even after being threatened by Goliath.

And the Philistine came on and drew near unto David; and the man that bare the shield went before him.

And when the Philistine looked about, and saw David, he disdained him: for he was but a youth, and ruddy, and of a fair countenance.

111

> And the Philistine said unto David, Am I a dog, that thou comest to me with staves? And the Philistine cursed David by his gods.
>
> And the Philistine said to David, Come to me, and I will give thy flesh unto the fowls of the air, and to the beasts of the field.
>
> Then said David to the Philistine, Thou comest to me with a sword, and with a spear, and with a shield: but I come to thee in the name of the Lord of hosts, the God of the armies of Israel, whom thou hast defied.
>
> 1 Samuel 17:41-45

David *said* something. Remember Jesus said in Mark 11:23,

> Whosoever shall say unto this mountain, Be thou removed, and be thou cast into the sea; and shall not doubt in his heart, but shall believe that those things which he saith shall come to pass; he shall have whatsoever he saith.

Goliath was a mountain for David, but David spoke to his mountain. He was framing his world with the Word of God.

> This day will the Lord deliver thee into mine hand; and I will smite thee, and take thine head from thee; and I will give the carcases of the host of the Philistines this day unto the fowls of the air, and to the wild beasts of the earth; that all the earth may know that there is a God in Israel.
>
> And all this assembly shall know that the Lord saveth not with sword and spear: for the battle is the Lord's, and he will give you into our hands.　　1 Samuel 17:46,47

Now, in the natural, it doesn't look like any deliverance is coming. Here is a boy with a slingshot and he's challenging a giant who is wearing a helmet and shield! Goliath was dressed for battle, and he laughed at the little boy with a slingshot and a bag of rocks. But David was using weapons that Goliath couldn't see. David was fighting with the Word of God.

> And it came to pass, when the Philistine arose, and came and drew nigh to meet David, that David hasted, and ran toward the army to meet the Philistine.
>
> And David put his hand in his bag, and took thence a stone, and slang it, and smote the Philistine in his forehead, that the stone sunk into his forehead; and he fell upon his face to the earth.
>
> 1 Samuel 17:48,49

David framed his world. Before he ever fought Goliath, he called out what the outcome would be. He called things that be not as though they were. (Rom. 4:17.) By faith, David said, "The Lord is going to give you into my hands today, Goliath, and I'm going to cut off your head!"

If you read the entire account, you'll find that it happened just as David said it would. David said it, and God brought it to pass. David put that stone into his slingshot and took aim, and God saw to it that it landed in the right place—the giant's forehead!

Receiving From God Is Not a Hit-or-Miss Proposition

When you frame your world with the Word of God, you ought to get an answer every time. When you operate in the faith of God, it's not a hit-or-miss agreement. God wants us to be successful in our praying and in our saying. If He didn't want us to succeed, He wouldn't have given us a pattern by which we could frame our world.

But He did give us a pattern: God would say something, and whatever He said came to pass. And when our thinking and believing line up with His Word, whatever *we* say can come to pass too!

8

Loose Your Faith
and Move Your Mountains!

Throughout His Word, God has given us the means to have faith and to use our faith to obtain what we need and desire. He has not left us helpless or without hope.

How Faith Comes

Romans 10 gives us excellent insight into how faith comes and how faith is exercised. Or we could say that it gives us insight into how to turn our faith loose.

> But what saith it? The word is nigh thee, even in thy mouth, and in thy heart: that is, the word of faith, which we preach;
>
> That if thou shalt confess with thy mouth the Lord Jesus, and shalt believe in thine heart that God hath raised him from the dead, thou shalt be saved.

> For with the heart man believeth unto righteousness; and with
> the mouth confession is made unto salvation....
>
> So then faith cometh by hearing, and hearing by the word of
> God.   Romans 10:8-10,17

We know from reading verse 17 that faith comes by hearing, and hearing by the Word of God. Then, in using or exercising faith, Paul talked about the heart-and-mouth connection in three places: (1) *The word is...in thy mouth, and in thy heart.* (v. 8); (2) *Thou shalt confess with thy mouth...and believe in thine heart.* (v. 9); and (3) *With the heart man believeth unto righteousness; and with the mouth confession is made unto salvation* (v. 10).

In this one passage, we can see that the way to *get* faith is by hearing the Word of God over and over again, thereby getting it into your heart. We also see that the way to *use*, or *exercise*, faith is by confessing with your mouth the Word that's in your heart.

I talked about it in detail before, but notice again that the *heart* is involved in *having* faith, or in *believing*. The *mouth* is involved in *using* faith, or in *saying*. Jesus Himself bears this out in the Gospels, where He talks about the connection between the heart and the mouth.

> For verily I say unto you, That whosoever shall say unto
> this mountain [you "say" with your mouth], Be thou removed, and
> be thou cast into the sea; and shall not doubt in his heart, but
> shall believe [in his heart] that those things which he saith shall
> come to pass; he shall have whatsoever he saith.
>
> Mark 11:23

In this verse, Jesus gives us a pointed, precise and powerful illustration of Matthew 12:34,35 in action. Matthew 12:34,35 says, **Out of the abundance of the heart the mouth speaketh. A good man out of the good treasure of the heart bringeth forth good things.**

In these verses Jesus was talking about believing and speaking; He was talking about the heart and the mouth.

What Is *Your* Mountain?

Do you believe that the word *whosoever* in that verse includes you? I tell you emphatically, yes, it does! Now consider the word *mountain.* I don't believe that Jesus was talking about a literal mountain of dirt, sand and rock. I believe He used the word *mountain* as an analogy to teach us that whenever a circumstance becomes a mountain in our lives, we can tell it to move and it will have to obey us if our believing is right.

Now what did Jesus say we are tell our mountain? We are to *say* to it: **...Be thou removed, and be thou cast into the sea....**

But there's more involved in the process than just saying words. The rest of the verse gives another qualification: **...and shall not doubt in his heart, but shall believe that those things which he saith shall come to pass; he shall have whatsoever he saith.**

Where did Jesus say we are not to doubt? In our *hearts.* Notice He didn't say anything about not doubting in our *heads.*

Do you know that you can have faith in your heart at the same time you have doubt in your head? Yes, you can. But when you keep your thoughts aligned with what you believe in your heart, your heart will whip your head in battle every time. On the contrary, if you align your thoughts with things that are contrary to the Word, your head is going to take over and dominate your spirit.

It is impossible in this life to stop the enemy from making suggestions to you, even though you know the Word and you're believing God. The devil is still going to make suggestions to you, give you wrong impressions and toy with your emotions. That's his job, and he's good at it! He is trying to discourage you about what you're believing for. He's trying to influence you and get you out of your faith and into operating from your heart and then your head.

Then if the devil can get you to start confessing what's in your head—which is based on what you feel, hear and see—you will begin to frame your world in the wrong way and with the wrong words.

How To Use Your Shield of Faith

I don't mind having the enemy shoot fiery darts at me, as long as I know how to hold up the shield of faith, because Ephesians 6:16 promises that the shield of faith can quench every fiery dart of the wicked. I know the darts are coming; they come to us all. But if you are using the shield of faith, those darts will just clank against that shield as they try to get to you. But they can't. They can't because you're using the shield of faith. You're saying, or confessing with your mouth, the Word of God that you believe in your heart, and you are keeping that shield up so no fiery darts can get past it.

But I also know that if you *don't* confess with your mouth the Word of God that you believe in your heart, you then leave yourself wide open as prey for the enemy.

Notice again that Matthew 12:34,35 and Mark 11:23 deal with the heart. They don't say anything about the head or the mind. If you try to deal with your head or your thought life to the exclusion of the Word, you're dealing just as a natural man. You need to deal as a spiritual man, because there is an enemy out there who is skillful at bringing doubts to your mind, and you have to do something with those thoughts as soon as they come. Why? Because the devil is after the Word; he's after your faith.

You have to deal with these wrong thoughts before they get down into your spirit. If you contemplate, court or "keep company with" the thoughts the devil brings, eventually, he is going to move from the formal living room to the family room and then to the innermost room of your heart. He's going to try to mess with that seed of the Word that you have planted in your heart. He's going to try to influence your thinking and your believing so he can change what you're confessing.

The Power of the Tongue

There's power in words, and especially in God's Word. What you consistently say, whether good or bad, will have a great impact on your life. That's why it's so necessary to speak good words.

> **Death and life are in the power of the tongue: and they that love it shall eat the fruit thereof.**
>
> Proverbs 18:21

You can either speak life to your situations and circumstances or you can speak death to them, and most people would agree that life is better than death. In other words, they prefer having life, not death, rule and reign in their lives. But choosing life over death is only the beginning. In order to speak life into your circumstances, you're going to have to know how to do it. When you learn how to properly speak to circumstances, you will begin framing your life with the Word of God.

Most of the time when you talk about death, people think you're talking about someone dying and being buried in a graveyard somewhere. But there are other kinds of death. Some people have many "graveyards" in their lives, because they are speaking death over their circumstances. Death in the form of failure and defeat is reigning in their lives because of the power of their tongue. They are experiencing the fruit of their own words, and it's death in whatever area they're speaking it.

Let me show you an Old Testament example of the power of the tongue. In Numbers 13 and 14 we find the account of the

twelve spies sent from the twelve tribes to spy out the land God
had promised to give the children of Israel.

And the Lord spake unto Moses, saying, Send thou men,
that they may search the land of Canaan, which I give unto the
children of Israel: of every tribe of their fathers shall ye send a
man, every one a ruler among them.

...And Moses sent them to spy out the land of Canaan, and
said unto them, Get you up this way southward, and go up into
the mountain: and see the land, what it is; and the people that
dwelleth therein, whether they be strong or weak, few or many;
and what the land is that they dwell in, whether it be good or
bad; and what cities they be that they dwell in, whether in tents,
or in strongholds; and what the land is, whether it be fat or
lean, whether there be wood therein, or not. And be ye of good
courage, and bring of the fruit of the land.

Now the time was the time of the firstripe grapes. So they
went up, and searched the land from the wilderness of Zin unto
Rehob, as men come to Hamath. And they ascended by the
south, and came unto Hebron; where Ahiman, Sheshai, and
Talmai, the children of Anak, were. (Now Hebron was built
seven years before Zoan in Egypt.)

And they came unto the brook of Eshcol, and cut down
from thence a branch with one cluster of grapes, and they bare
it between two upon a staff; and they brought of the pomegran-
ates, and of the figs.

...And they returned from searching of the land after forty
days. And they went and came to Moses, and to Aaron, and to

all the congregation of the children of Israel, unto the wilderness of Paran, to Kadesh; and brought back word unto them, and unto all the congregation, and shewed them the fruit of the land.

And they told him, and said, We came unto the land whither thou sentest us, and surely it floweth with milk and honey; and this is the fruit of it. Nevertheless the people be strong that dwell in the land, and the cities are walled, and very great: and moreover we saw the children of Anak there. The Amalekites dwell in the land of the south: and the Hittites, and the Jebusites, and the Amorites, dwell in the mountains: and the Canaanites dwell by the sea, and by the coast of Jordan.

And Caleb stilled the people before Moses, and said, Let us go up at once, and possess it; for we are well able to overcome it.

But the men that went up with him said, We be not able to go up against the people; for they are stronger than we.

And they brought up an evil report of the land which they had searched unto the children of Israel, saying, The land, through which we have gone to search it, is a land that eateth up the inhabitants thereof; and all the people that we saw in it are men of a great stature. And there we saw the giants, the sons of Anak, which come of the giants: and we were in our own sight as grasshoppers, and so we were in their sight.

Numbers 13:1,2,17-23,25-33

Reading this passage carefully, we can see that twelve men were in the same place, seeing the same thing, yet some of them saw things differently. Why? Because ten men saw with their natural eyes; the other two were seeing with the eyes of faith.

Ten of the spies saw the fruit of the land, and they saw that it was good. But they saw the giants there too. I'm sure the other two spies, Joshua and Caleb, saw the same giants. But they had a different report. What made the difference in what each group received? Their confession—what they *said* made the difference.

Ten spies *said, "We saw the land where you sent us, and it did flow with milk and honey. But the people who live there are strong! And the cities have walls around them, and the children of Anak are there"* (vv. 27,28).

Joshua and Caleb said something different, however. They said, *"Let's go and possess the land at once. We're more than able to overcome it"* (v. 30).

Your Confession Will Set Your Landmarks

Joshua and Caleb set the landmarks of their lives by what they said. They said, in essence, "No matter what the giants there looked like that we saw with our physical eyes, we're going in there to take the land. God has given us Canaan, and into Canaan we shall go!"

Notice the stark contrast between what the two groups said. Joshua and Caleb said, **Let us go up at once, and possess it; for we are well able to overcome it.**

The other group said, **We be not able to go up against the people; for they are stronger than we.**

One group said, "We are well able." The other group said, "We are *not* able."

Now look at something else the second, unbelieving group said:

> And there we saw the giants, the sons of Anak, which come of the giants: and we were in our own sight as grasshoppers, and so we were in their sight.

First, how did they know how they appeared in the sight of their enemy? They said, "We were in our own sight as grasshoppers. So that's how we were in their sight too." There is another Old Testament verse which says, **As he** [a man] **thinketh in his heart, so is he** (Prov. 23:7).

Christians today have had a grasshopper mentality. The world has been telling us that we're nobodies, and we've believed them. We've been out selling raffle tickets trying to help out our churches. We've said, "Take a chance. Give a dollar donation for God's poor church."

Many pastors have had a grasshopper mentality. They've refused to walk by faith, and they've refused to teach their people to walk by faith. As a result, they've produced a bunch of little grasshoppers just like themselves.

We need to dare to receive all God has for us. We need to get rid of that grasshopper mentality and start seeing ourselves as the overcomers that we are in Christ.

> What shall we then say to these things? If God be for us,
> who can be against us?
>
> He that spared not his own Son, but delivered him up for
> us all, how shall he not with him also freely give us all
> things?.... Nay, in all these things we are more than conquerors
> through him that loved us.
>
> Romans 8:31,32,37

We are not grasshoppers. As we put God's Word into our
hearts, we will see ourselves as God sees us. First John 4:4 says,
Greater is he that is in you, than he that is in the world. Philippians 4:13 says, **I can do all things through Christ which
strengtheneth me.** Mark 9:23 says, **If thou canst believe, all
things are possible to him that believeth.**

Keep confessing those things until they become reality in your
heart. Then go forward with the Word of God in your heart and
mouth and watch God do great things in your life.

Some Christians are always wishing or hoping things would get
better in their lives. They'll say, for example, "Mr. Smith has such a
nice family. I wish my family were like that."

"Why don't you start confessing the Word over your family?"
I'll ask.

"Well, I would, but my husband is always acting up. He'll never
come around."

"Why don't you fight, then?" I ask.

I'm not talking about physically fighting with your family—with flesh and blood. I'm talking about rising up in faith and confessing the Word of God. For example, don't confess your husband as he is now. Confess him as you want him to be and as God, according to His Word, wants him to be. If you will have in life what you confess, why not confess good things? Why not confess the Bible?

Let's look at what happened in Numbers. What were the end results of the confessions of the spies after one group said, "We are well able," and the other group said, "We be not able"? The crowd sided with the ten unbelieving spies.

> **And they** [the ten spies] **brought up an evil report of the land...unto the children of Israel, saying, The land, through which we have gone to search it, is a land that eateth up the inhabitants thereof; and all the people that we saw in it are men of a great stature.**
>
> **And there we saw the giants, the sons of Anak, which come of the giants: and we were in our own sight as grasshoppers, and so we were in their sight.**
>
> **And all the congregation lifted up their voice, and cried; and the people wept that night.**
>
> Numbers 13:32,33; 14:1

I tell you, if you hang with the wrong crowd, they will hinder your faith. Joshua and Caleb had faith, but by having to be with those other "skeptics," it took them forty years to do what they believed they could do at that moment.

Some Christians will say, "I only want to go back to my old life and be with my old friends." That is a dangerous attitude, because those old friends are going to hinder you spiritually if they're not walking with God. They're going to deter you or keep you altogether out of the things of God.

The children of Israel kept Joshua and Caleb out of the Promised Land for forty years. They had to wait until an entire generation died out before they could enter into what God had for them. For forty long years, they wandered around in the desert.

The ten spies and the other Israelites had said, "We be not able." God became angry and said, "All right then. Have it your way. You can have what you say."

> And all the children of Israel murmured against Moses and against Aaron: and the whole congregation said unto them, Would God that we had died in the land of Egypt! or would God we had died in this wilderness!
>
> And wherefore hath the Lord brought us unto this land, to fall by the sword, that our wives and our children should be a prey? were it not better for us to return into Egypt?
>
> **Numbers 14:2,3**

Look at God's response to them after they said, "Would God that we had died in this wilderness!"

> ...As truly as I live, saith the Lord, as ye have spoken in mine ears, so will I do to you:

> Your carcases shall fall in this wilderness; and all that were numbered of you, according to your whole number, from twenty years old and upward, which have murmured against me,
>
> Doubtless ye shall not come into the land, concerning which I sware to make you dwell therein, save Caleb the son of Jephunneh, and Joshua the son of Nun.
>
> Numbers 14:28-30

The ten spies brought back an evil report of unbelief, and they received the fruit of their lips. In other words, they got what they said. But on the positive side, even though it took Joshua and Caleb longer to enter into because of their unbelieving brothers, they did eventually enter into the Promised Land. They got what they said. And you can have what *you* say too.

'Refrain Your Tongue From Evil'

Now let me show you a New Testament Scripture that deals with the power of the tongue. First Peter 3:10 says, **For he that will love life, and see good days, let him refrain his tongue from evil, and his lips that they speak no guile.**

I want to love life and see good days. How about you? What are good days? Good days are when you're full of joy and peace and you're in fellowship with God. Good days are when you're healthy and have plenty of money. Good days are when your family relationships are right.

The church has been seeing some bad days, but this verse tells us what to do about it: *Let him refrain his tongue from evil.*

Do you know some of the things that the Bible calls evil? Doubt and unbelief are two of them. We just read that the ten unbelieving spies brought back an evil report, and God called their unbelief "evil."

Do you want to love life and see good days? Well, the instructions are simple: Refrain your tongue from evil, and let your lips speak no guile. If you obey that command, you will possess the love of life and see many good days.

I'm talking about how to loose your faith and move your mountains, and the way to accomplish that can be found right under your nose: You release your faith with your mouth, with what you say.

> **For this commandment which I command thee this day, it is not hidden from thee, neither is it far off. It is not in heaven, that thou shouldest say, Who shall go up for us to heaven, and bring it unto us, that we may hear it, and do it? Neither is it beyond the sea, that thou shouldest say, Who shall go over the sea for us, and bring it unto us, that we may hear it, and do it? But the word is very nigh unto thee, in thy mouth, and in thy heart, that thou mayest do it. See, I have set before thee this day life and good, and death and evil.**
>
> **Deuteronomy 30:11-15**

The Word is in your heart and mouth that you may do it. God doesn't want the Word to simply lie dormant in your heart. He wants you to *say* it, and He also wants you to act on your faith!

> **In that I command thee this day to love the Lord thy God, to walk in his ways, and to keep his commandments and his statutes and his judgments, that thou mayest live and multiply: and the Lord thy God shall bless thee in the land whither thou goest to possess it.**
>
> **...I call heaven and earth to record this day against you, that I have set before you life and death, blessing and cursing: therefore choose life, that both thou and thy seed may live: that thou mayest love the Lord thy God, and that thou mayest obey his voice, and that thou mayest cleave unto him: for he is thy life, and the length of thy days: that thou mayest dwell in the land which the Lord sware unto thy fathers, to Abraham, to Isaac, and to Jacob, to give them.**
>
> Deuteronomy 30:16,19,20

Let's look at the words which concern loving the Lord. If you love Him, you're going to obey Him. You're going to keep His Word in your heart and in your mouth for the purpose of honoring Him and of having it go well with you: **For he is thy life, and the length of thy days: that thou mayest dwell in the land** (v. 20).

What land is this verse talking about? For the Israelites, it was talking about a physical land that flowed with milk and honey—the land of Canaan. But for us, our "promised land" is what Christ provided for us in His death, burial and resurrection. We are a chosen generation which has been called out of darkness into the kingdom of light. (1 Peter 2:9.)

We're in this physical world, but we're not of it. (John 17:15,16.) We've been placed in another world; our citizenship is in heaven. We are to live by heavenly principles, and one of those principles is that of framing our world with the Word of God.

As I said, don't confess what you don't have; confess what you desire to have. Don't talk about what you can't do; talk about what you *can* do through Christ who strengthens you.

It's up to you now. It's not up to God anymore; He has done His part. He sent Jesus. The Holy Ghost indwells you, and you have God's Word. Use it to frame your world.

What you say out of your mouth is either going to produce life in your circumstances or it will produce death. You can speak words of life, you can agree with God and renew your mind with His Word so that your thinking, believing and speaking are right, or you can talk contrary to God's Word and permit death to rule in your life.

I made up my mind that I'm going to speak life to my situations and circumstances. I am going to find out what God has to say about me and my situation, and I'm going to say what *He* says.

In every circumstance that arises in my life, I go to the Word of God and find out what God says I should do, and then I do it. You see, the promises of God are conditional. In other words, we have a part to play in the outcome. But when we do our part, I assure you, the Father God will do His part.

There are changes and adjustments we have to make if we want to get in on this system of framing our world with the Word, but we can start today. There are wrong ways of thinking, believing and speaking in our lives that we have to undo. It's going to take some effort and some work on our part, and I don't mean just now and then. I'm talking about putting some effort and work into it every day.

But the benefits of framing our world far outweigh the work it will take to get there. We want to think right, believe right and confess right, because the consequences of a wrong confession can be devastating to our lives.

When you speak doubt, defeat and destruction to your life, you will eventually produce doubt, defeat and destruction. But today you can curse the wrong words you've spoken over your life and begin to speak the words you're supposed to speak. It's a process. Things won't change overnight just because you decide to change. It will take time. You may have to work on it for a while, but you'll see that, finally, you will reach the point where each time you open your mouth to speak, your heart will be in agreement. Power will be produced to frame your life concerning whatever it is you're speaking.

Begin today to speak life to your body, to your family relationships, to your job and to your finances. You can also speak words of life over your spouse. And you single people can even speak words of life over the mate you're believing for!

Your Words Can Imprison You

Many want to argue that what you say, your confession, is not important. But I think we can see from the Word that what you say is very important. We know that God framed the world with His words, and we will frame our world with words too.

Let's look at another verse that illustrates the importance of a good confession. Proverbs 6:2 says, **Thou art snared** [or trapped] **with the words of thy mouth, thou art taken with the words of thy mouth.**

Remember we read Proverbs 18:21: **Death and life are in the power of the tongue....** In light of Proverbs 6:2, which we just read, we could read that verse this way: "Being trapped or not being trapped are in the power of the tongue."

Notice something else about Proverbs 6:2. It says that you are snared and taken with the words of your mouth. So framing your world is up to you. It's not up to your husband or wife, it's not up to your parents or grandparents, it's not up to your pastor, your friends or your fellow church members. It's up to *you!*

You see, framing your world is an individual thing. As it says in Matthew 12:37, **For by thy words thou shalt be justified, and by thy words thou shalt be condemned.** So it's not *someone else's* words that will justify or condemn you or bring you life or death; it's your *own* words.

Similarly, you can't frame someone else's world with your words, no matter how much you would like to be able to. In general, your words will affect only *your* life, not someone else's, because his faith must be involved too. In other words, you may be believing and speaking one thing about him, and at the same time he may be believing and speaking another thing entirely. His life has more to do with his own faith than with your faith or anyone else's faith.

Now that's not to say that you can never use your faith for someone else because, in certain cases, a baby Christian can be carried on another's faith. But, in general, you need to have your thinking, believing and speaking right for yourself in order to frame your world, and the other person needs to have his thinking, believing and speaking right for himself to frame *his* world.

But, thank God, you *can* frame your own world! You can choose life or death by the words you speak. I choose to speak life: I choose to have health; I choose to have wealth; I choose to have joy and peace. You see, I have a choice! In many ways it's my choice that helps determine what happens in my life.

As I said, you will never completely stop your head from going against the Word of God. But you can stop it from having any kind of authority in your life by thinking right, believing right and speaking right.

Remember what it says in Mark 11:23:

> For verily I say unto you, That whosoever shall say unto this mountain, Be thou removed, and be thou cast into the sea; and shall not doubt in his heart, but shall believe that those things which he saith shall come to pass; he shall have whatsoever he saith.

Look at that phrase, ...**and shall not doubt in his heart....** The thing that keeps doubt from coming into your heart is having the Word in your heart. When you hide the Word in your heart, faith comes. Psalm 119:130 says, **The entrance of thy words giveth light....**

When the Word dawns on your heart, faith is automatically present. You then have the ability to tell your mountain to be removed and cast into the sea. Then if you don't doubt in your heart, but shall believe that what you said will come to pass, you shall have it.

The problems come when you doubt in your heart. Notice I didn't say that problems come when you doubt in your *head,* because we know a person can have faith in his heart and doubt in his head. But that doesn't mean you should simply let doubt run rampant in your head. No, remember I said you need to cast down evil or wrong thoughts—thoughts that exalt themselves against the knowledge of God, or against God's Word.

When doubt comes, if you let it stay in your head, it is not going to be content to stay there. It's going to travel to another room in your house. Then, it's going to go down into your heart.

And if doubt gets into your heart, it will get into your mouth, and then your life will become a life of doubt. You will be speaking words of death, not life, and the result is that you will be framing your world with the wrong words.

9

Make Confessions of Faith

We already talked about casting down wrong thoughts, but let me share with you a trick of the enemy that many people fall for. They're trying to frame their world, but perhaps in the area of health and healing, this thought might come to them: "Well, Grandma had arthritis. Mama had arthritis. I'm probably going to have arthritis too." Or, "High blood pressure runs in my family. I know I'm going to have high blood pressure."

Those thoughts come, and because they are statements of the facts in the natural, people often don't think they need to stand against them. They think that because a certain sickness or disease runs in their family, they're susceptible to it also.

But think about it! If you're born again, you're in the family of God! You're not in any other family, from the standpoint of being susceptible to sickness and disease. Certainly those things may be true in the natural. Maybe Mama and Grandma *did* have arthritis or some other disease. But you're in another family! There's no arthritis or high blood pressure or *any* sickness and disease in the family of God!

You have to go against the grain about that concept. You may even have to go against all of your family members about it. But you need to keep your thinking, believing and speaking straight concerning healing so you can frame your world in that area and walk and live in divine health.

You need to have the attitude, "Even if all ninety-five members of my family are sick, I'm going to frame my world with the Word of God that says I don't have to be sick. God's Word says that I can speak to my mountain of sickness and tell it to be removed from my life and cast into the sea. And I can have what I say. I can frame my world with God's Word."

You Can Confess in the Wrong Direction

Instead of confessing what they want or need, people often confess what they have, what they don't have or what they see and feel. They confess lack, so lack gains ascendency in their lives. They are holding themselves back because of what they're confessing with their own mouths.

People who are always talking about what they can't do, aren't able to do or what they'll never have won't even rise above that position in life. Their words are words of doubt and unbelief that give the devil access into their lives. Their words give the devil something to work with, and although God would like to help them, they tie His hands.

When you confess Satan's ability to hinder you and keep you from success, you give Satan dominion over you. Some people are always talking about what the devil is doing, and what they should be talking about is what God is doing. They should be giving God, not the devil, something to work with in their lives.

What is it that we should be confessing then? Romans 10:9 gives us the answer:

> **If thou shalt confess with thy mouth the Lord Jesus, and shalt believe in thine heart that God hath raised him from the dead, thou shalt be saved.**

In every situation and circumstance, we should be confessing the lordship of Jesus. When you confess the lordship of Jesus over every situation, Jesus becomes bigger in your life than the problem. He is then able to exercise His lordship in your life and bring things to pass for you.

You will not rise above your confession. But your confession, based on the reality of God's Word, will take you to places you only dreamed of in the past.

I know that's true in my own life. Before our new church auditorium was built, I used to stand on our property, look over acres of green grass and call the church building into existence. I didn't have any money at the time; I made my confession based on God's Word alone. I knew what He'd called me to do, and I knew I couldn't fully accomplish it without that building. So before I ever saw anything with my natural eyes, I began to see that church with the eyes of faith.

Before we ever broke ground for the church, I talked about what it was going to look like. I talked about the carpet, the chairs, the speakers' platform, the foyers, the classrooms and so forth. I talked about the parking lot and about all the cars that would be parked beside the highway, because so many people wanted to attend our church! I envisioned people driving from all around to come to Darrow to hear the Word of God preached.

We only had about sixty-five members at the time all that occurred, but everything came to pass just as I'd said! Before long, we built that beautiful new auditorium. *And it's paid for!*

The point I want to make is this: The confession of our mouths that has grown out of faith in our hearts will absolutely beat the devil every time! There is no person, place, thing, entity or being anywhere that can stop God's Word from residing in our hearts and being spoken from our mouths.

The Role of Confession

What is the role of confession? As I said, the confession of the mouth that is born of faith in the heart will produce God's power to change circumstances and to work wonders in your life.

But confession without any faith in the heart is powerless; it's useless. You might be wondering, *Well, what if I don't believe in my heart? Should I still confess the Word of God?* Yes, because with your lips, you can make confessions unto faith. In other words, as you say God's Word over and over again, faith can be built in your heart where before there wasn't any faith.

You can speak God's Word so much that it will eventually affect your heart, and you will begin believing it. In fact, many times the confessions we make are actually doing nothing more than getting us ready to confess! They're putting faith into our hearts so we can make confessions that will produce power.

That's thoroughly scriptural, because the Bible says that faith comes by hearing, and hearing by the Word of God. (Rom. 10:17.) That verse implies to me that faith comes by hearing the Word of God spoken over and over again.

So keep yourself in a position to hear the Word of God. Keep saying it over and over so you'll hear it and begin to believe it. Then once you believe it, God will step in and work on your behalf.

Good or bad, you will have what you say in life. You will either rise or fall to the level of your confession.

10

The 'Wait' of Faith

If you have your thinking right, your believing right and your speaking right, you will understand that it's not what you see that should determine for you whether the Word is working. It's not by your home or your possessions that you know if you're successful. The way you can know that your world is being framed by the Word is by what's in your heart and by what you're saying. You will know in your heart that everything is eventually going to line up with the Word.

I was once asked, "But, Reverend Thompson, how long will it be before it happens?"

As long as it takes. Just stay with it. Stay with God's Word. Jeremiah 1:12 says, **I** [God] **will hasten my word to perform it.** Another translation says that God watches over His Word to perform it. So no matter how things look, if you're speaking the

Word of God in faith, don't quit! Stay in faith, and everything will be all right.

In the natural, a pregnant woman carries a child in her body for approximately nine months before giving birth. Now, she doesn't go to the doctor after four months and say, "I want my baby today!" No, the duration of her pregnancy is nine months.

Being pregnant for nine months is not an easy job. I mean, the woman gets big, especially toward the end of her pregnancy. She has trouble tying her shoes—if she can even see her feet! She feels awkward and uncomfortable. Don't let anyone tell you it's easy to carry a baby inside you for nine months!

But a pregnant woman doesn't question the fact that it takes nine months to finally give birth to that child she's carrying. She accepts it as a natural fact of life. Then the delivery day comes, and the child comes forth.

Get 'Pregnant' With the Word

I'm using this analogy to teach you something about faith and patience, because often spiritual things come about in ways that are parallel to physical things.

If you are believing God for something, try to envision yourself as being "pregnant" with what you're believing for. Then be prepared to "incubate" whatever that is for however long it takes to bring it forth. Absorb the Word of God as a seed into your heart or spirit throughout that gestation period and just carry that "pregnancy" through to the birth.

I mean, if there was something a pregnant woman shouldn't do because it would be detrimental to her unborn child, in most instances she wouldn't do it because she wants her child to be healthy and well.

Likewise, you need to care for the seed of the Word of God that you have in your heart. Hold fast to your confession of faith for the full duration of the waiting period so that seed can come forth in its fullness. What I believe the Holy Ghost is saying in this analogy is that just as a woman carries a child for nine months and anticipates her date of delivery with joy, give the Word of God in your heart equal time to develop and anticipate its manifestation with joy.

Now I'm not saying that what you're believing for will literally take nine months. But from start to finish—from the time that Word gets in your heart to the time it manifests itself—there will be a certain duration of time. I don't know how long that time will be for you, but I believe it can be sped up by keeping your thinking, believing and speaking in line with the Word and by keeping your heart right, especially in the areas of walking in love and forgiveness toward others.

When some people are believing God for something, they want Him to instantly jump to it and—*pop*—bring forth their answer as quickly as a jack-in-the-box pops up when the lid is lifted!

So many times we want something *right now*. For example, have you ever opened the bottom of a box of cereal so you could get the prize inside first? Or have you ever turned the box upside down and shaken it to try to get the prize to the top? We want to somehow get to the prize first, because we want it *now*—not later.

God wants us to "eat the cereal" day by day, and He wants us to begin at the top of the box! We need to get a little experience with the "box" and its contents before we reach the bottom of the box. That way we'll know how to handle the "prize" when we get to it.

What Happens Between *Saying* and *Seeing*

Whosoever shall say unto this mountain, Be thou removed, and be thou cast into the sea; and shall not doubt in his heart, but shall believe that those things which he saith shall come to pass; he shall have whatsoever he saith.

Mark 11:23

When using this Scripture, most people don't realize that there's going to be a span of time between the time they *say* something and the time they *have* it or *see* it. But the answer doesn't always come automatically. You have to hold fast to what you're saying, and you can't let situations or circumstances change your confession.

If we can accept the word of man regarding things in our daily lives, we certainly should have the assurance that we can accept the

Word of God. After all, God Himself will stand behind His Word to make it good in our lives.

Most of us will work diligently on our jobs all week with no proof whatsoever that we're going to get a paycheck on Friday. Yet our employer said that Friday is payday, so we work every day, never worrying whether or not we'll get paid. We accept it as fact.

We need to show the same consideration for God's Word and hold fast to saying what God says.

There Is No Neutral Ground

Many people might say, "Well, I don't want to get involved with all that confession business. I just want to be a good Christian."

If you decide to remain neutral on the issue of faith and confession, the devil is going to step up and make some confessions *for* you. His demons are going to show up on your doorstep with a package of goods that you do not want.

Framing your world with the Word of God is not a game. It is a war, and in a war there is no neutral zone. There is no place you can go to separate yourself from the warfare that's going on over your faith in the Word.

You need to actively protect your faith and learn to use it. If you don't, the devil might let you "coast" for maybe ten years as you become complacent in your faith. And then in the eleventh year, he could wipe you and your family out because you refused to stay ready to resist him and to frame your world with God's Word.

It is your responsibility to see that your thinking, believing and speaking are right. If you don't take that responsibility, the devil is going to think your thoughts for you. He'll actually have you believing what he wants you to believe. And he'll eventually have you confessing what he wants you to confess, framing your world with the wrong words and letting him have dominion over you.

If you're not renewing your mind with the Word, other things are going to get into your mind and heart. Then those things are going to find their way to your mouth. And when they do, you're going to speak those things out, and you'll wonder, *Where in the world did that come from?*

But when you get enough Word in you, every time a negative circumstance arises, the Word will automatically rise up out of your spirit, and the first thing that will register with your mind will be, *What has God said about this?*

I exhort you to align your thinking, your believing and your speaking with the Word of God and then hold fast to your confession of faith. Don't waver in it because God, who framed the worlds with His own words, is faithful to see you through if you just won't quit. It may not happen immediately, and it may not happen as quickly as you'd like—but stick with it. You *can* frame your world with the Word!

11

How To Frame Your Financial World With the Word of God
Part 1

God spoke to me many years ago about how we can frame our world with His Word. God framed the world with His own Word (Heb. 11:3), and our individual world will also be framed and formed by His Word in our heart and in our mouth. The circumstances of our lives are largely a product of words we have spoken in the past. But we can look forward with great anticipation to a bright and beautiful future as we direct our future with words of faith and power from the Word of God.

First, a Foundation

What exactly is involved in this process of framing our world for finances? As it is with any building project, we must first have a foundation of absolute conviction that prosperity is God's will for us. Then we complete the framing—and, lastly, we add the finishing touches.

Often, in laying a proper foundation suitable to support and sustain the framing process for financial wealth, some things in our lives have to be dealt with—individually, but also in the Body of Christ. In the Body of Christ at large, there is *mass, organized, and "incorporated and approved" ignorance* concerning covenant wealth! So many believers are suffering financially, but they shouldn't be suffering! They love God, and they give into His Kingdom, but they are not receiving their harvest as they should. They simply don't understand God's will concerning financial prosperity.

Time for Change

We should realize that it's time for change when everyone in the house has to work to make ends meet, and we're living from paycheck to paycheck. No one is minding the house, and instead of getting ahead, things seem to be getting worse, because we're spinning your wheels, so to speak. We're tired, discouraged, and discontented.

Financial stress affects us physically too. It is a medical fact that stress directly and indirectly contributes to physical diseases, such as heart attack, stroke, diabetes, and other maladies. Also, when we're spending most of our day working and trying to keep up with all of our payments, other aspects of our lives are sacrificed. Perhaps we're not spending the time with our children that we should be spending. Oftentimes, children get into trouble, and one of the reasons is parental neglect, because the parents' time is being monopolized working all those jobs so the family can stay afloat financially.

So many aspects of our lives boil down to money. Many people have not yet recognized that most of their troubles can be traced back to a lack of finances. It's time to recognize the truth and then deal with it accordingly. It's time to start framing your financial world with the Word of God.

The Blessing of the Tithe

We've heard a lot of preaching and teaching on the blessing of the tithe. But there are many good Christians who tithe faithfully, yet they're still struggling financially. It's time for a "tithes manifestation"! It's time for tithers to receive the harvest from what they've sown in obedience to God. I believe that those who tithe, those who are actively working God's economic system, will begin to see great manifestations in the coming days. And right behind that, every step will be a step of increase. Walking from bedroom to kitchen, every step will be one of increase and blessing! God is going to open the windows of Heaven and pour us out blessings that we don't have room enough to receive (Mal. 3:10). But we need to rise up with supernatural expectation for these things to happen.

One purpose for this chapter is to address some of the ignorance that has plagued the Body of Christ concerning prosperity. Many have been in a backward situation in that they are walking far beneath their Blood-bought privileges. God calls them the "head," but they are living as though they are the "tail" (*see* Deuteronomy 28:13).

Let's look at a couple of scriptures in Ecclesiastes that point out something very important along this line. I believe the Holy Spirit will use it to open your eyes so you can turn around any "backward situation" in your life with the Word of God and begin framing your world to include prosperity.

> There is an evil which I have seen under the sun, as an error which proceedeth from the ruler:
>
> Folly is set in great dignity, and the rich sit in low place.
>
> I have seen servants upon horses, and princes walking as servants upon the earth.
>
> Ecclesiastes 10:5-7

The writer called the things he saw "evil" and "error." Then he proceeded to tell what it was that he saw: *folly and foolishness dignified* and *wealth and wisdom degraded* (v. 6), and *servants riding on horses* and *princes walking as servants* (v. 7).

Many Christians have been choked by the world's system, and they've gotten turned around in their finances. But they're not supposed to be the beggar at the gate of the rich man! They're supposed to own the gate so the world will see how rich our God is!

As the Body of Christ, we are not in our right place, experiencing the level of finances the Lord needs us to experience in order to carry out our assignment in the earth. We should see that fact as an "evil" and an "error," because God has desired that we experience great breakthroughs instead of year after year of struggling and barely getting by. The Lord will unravel some of these backward situations if we will receive and partake of it by faith. The way He will unravel them is with His wisdom. So instead of seeing evil and error under the sun, as Solomon did, we can see *evil, error, and* the solution if we will receive the wisdom of God.

A Heavenly Solution—Seven Keys To Framing Your Financial World

There are seven key factors that every believer urgently needs to know about how to change his financial situation God's way. I have utilized these key factors in my own experi-

ence in life, and they have consistently brought me into God's
financial blessing.

Number One: Doctrine

The first four of the seven keys to successfully framing
your world for finances come from Second Timothy 3:16,
which gives us an instructional format for framing our world.
Those four keys are (1) *doctrine*; (2) *reproof*; (3) *correction*; and (4)
instruction in righteousness. The last of the seven keys are (5)
wisdom; (6) *understanding*; and (7) *knowledge*.

**All scripture is given by inspiration of God, and is
profitable for doctrine, for reproof, for correction, for instruction in righteousness.**

2 Timothy 3:16

I had read this scripture hundreds of times, but the Lord
dealt with me about these four words: *doctrine, reproof, correction,*
and *instruction in righteousness*. These four elements that God's
Word brings forth are very important to any spiritual transaction. Why? **That the man of God may be perfect,
throughly furnished unto all good works** (2 Tim. 3:17).

Number one, every believer who wants to change his financial picture must understand *doctrine*. "Doctrine" refers to
God's precepts or to the established order of God. The
promises, the Covenant, and the Kingdom of God are all a
part of His established order. Whatever we're going to believe

and build upon concerning wealth, abundance, and increase must be found within that established order.

In other words, there are godly principles—spiritual laws—that we must follow after persistently if we are to increase financially. So first, we have to understand the principles through our study of the Word of God. When God's Word is quickened in our heart and faith comes, we don't have to know how we're going to increase or even how the laws of increase work. All we have to do is believe and trust and then do what God tells us to do. Walking in obedience is establishing the order of God in our lives. When we walk in obedience to the Word—to sound *doctrine*—we will see godly results.

We need to know what God says in His Word about wealth, and we need to obey that. We need to conform our thoughts, words, and deeds to His Word and His way of thinking. So what does God say about our income? What does God say about what we should have in life? I'm not talking about what *man* says we should have, but what *God* says.

The Bible says that we as believers are blessed with the blessing of Abraham (Gal. 3:14). God called Abraham, and God blessed and increased His covenant friend (James 2:23). God has called us too. And we are to walk in blessing and increase as we understand and partake of by faith the covenant we have entered into with God in Christ. That's why doctrine must be established in our lives. It's the divine order of God that prospers us, not our secular or academic backgrounds. The blessings of God must come through the realm of the Spirit, not through the realm of the flesh or natural man.

The first thing every believer needs to know is that it is God's will that he prospers. And then that believer needs to go to work establishing God's will and order in his life.

If you know that something isn't going the way it should go, you know that something in your life needs to be corrected so things can go the right way. God wants things to go right with you, because when His order is not being established concerning finances, it causes stress and pressure, not peace. God is not glorified when His children are weighted down by oppressive loads of anxiety and care.

It is the establishing of doctrine—of God's order—in people's lives that deals with the mass, organized, and "incorporated and approved" ignorance over wealth. Establishing ourselves in sound doctrine does away the question about whether God wants us to have it! We can have whatever His Word says we can have—abundant wealth without exception—if we will do things God's way, or according to His established order.

Talking about the established order of God, Second Corinthians 1:20-22 says,

> For all the promises of God in him are yea, and in him
> Amen, unto the glory of God by us.
>
> Now he which stablisheth us with you in Christ, and hath
> anointed us, is God.
>
> Who hath also sealed us, and given the earnest of the Spirit in
> our hearts.

God will establish you if you will let Him — if you will study His Word with an open and sincere heart and let the Holy Spirit open eyes of your understanding concerning the divine order for finances.

In the eyes of God, His people should be enjoying His highest and best in life. Haggai 2:8 says, **The silver is mine, and the gold is mine, saith the Lord of hosts.** Since the silver and gold in the earth are God's, why would He want His own children to live in poverty, lack, and want?

We just read that all the promises of God in Christ are "yes and amen." So we need to find out what the promises of God are concerning our finances and then establish those promises in our heart. We must know the truth of the Word and become fully persuaded about the truth so that we will be unsusceptible to lies and untruths. We can't do that by just taking other people's word for something; we must go to God's Word for ourselves.

A Sweatless Anointing

There is a financial anointing for the Body of Christ. That anointing encompasses the foundation, the framing, and the finishing touches of your financial future.

I am walking in that anointing, and I am telling you that it is a *sweatless* anointing. When you learn to cooperate with it, you don't have to work two or three jobs, go to bed late, get up early, and struggle, strive, and connive to make it in life.

Finances are not the problem — the problem is getting aligned with God's established order. When you learn the promises of God and you welcome and receive those promises, you become "sealed." You look at famine and laugh, because it cannot touch you. You know that financial stability and blessing are the will of God for you, and you will not be denied what is yours!

Without becoming sound in doctrine, establishing the will and order of God in your life, others will try to establish you on something else — on some other foundation, such as traditions of men. They will tell you that their way is the way you should go. If you're not established on the Word of God, you will end up going in a different direction, and you will cut yourself off from the promise of God for prosperity until you turn around and go in God's direction, establishing yourself on His Word.

The Spirit of Fear and the Voice of Authority

Psalm 112 paints a divine picture of the covenant riches of the righteous.

Praise ye the Lord. Blessed is the man that feareth the Lord, that delighteth greatly in his commandments.

His seed shall be mighty upon earth: the generation of the upright shall be blessed.

Wealth and riches shall be in his house: and his righteousness endureth for ever.

Unto the upright there ariseth light in the darkness: he is gracious, and full of compassion, and righteous.

A good man sheweth favour, and lendeth: he will guide his affairs with discretion.

Surely he shall not be moved for ever: the righteous shall be in everlasting remembrance.

He shall not be afraid of evil tidings: his heart is fixed, trusting in the Lord.

His heart is established, he shall not be afraid, until he see his desire upon his enemies.

He hath dispersed, he hath given to the poor; his righteousness endureth for ever; his horn shall be exalted with honour.

The wicked shall see it, and be grieved; he shall gnash with his teeth, and melt away: the desire of the wicked shall perish.

Psalm 112:1-10

Notice it says in verses 6 and 8 that the righteous person shall not be moved. He is established—*fixed*—because his heart trusts soundly in the Lord. This is a picture of the person who sees the Word of God as his final authority.

You cannot become established in doctrine unless you respect God's Word as the ultimate voice of authority in your life. But when you're established, or fixed, bad news does not affect you like it used to. And since it doesn't have any effect on you, it can't cause fear in your life. And since bad news can't cause fear in you, Satan can't use that bad news against you.

The spirit of fear is one of the greatest hindrances to the Body of Christ's walking in their God-given rights. The enemy will either try to make a person fear that he's going under and won't make it financially, or he'll try to convince a person that money is evil and that having money will draw him or her away from God. But when that person knows the truth and is established on sound doctrine, the devil's lies will be of no effect in the person's life.

Number Two: Reproof

All scripture is given by inspiration of God, and is profitable for doctrine, for reproof, for correction, for instruction in righteousness.

2 Timothy 3:16

Number two, every believer who wants to change his financial picture must understand *reproof*.

What is "reproof"? Reproof is similar in importance to doctrine in that it solidifies our conviction of the absolute truth of God's Word. Reproof proves out the Scripture, dismantling erroneous teaching and thinking in our lives. In other words, when the Word of God comes to you, it not only brings teaching of doctrine or the establishing of God's will and order, but if there is something in your life that needs to be dealt with, that same Word can deal with it and cause your spiritual roots to go down even deeper into the truth.

The Word of God can reprove you, and this is where many Christians "fall off." There are some things that are blocking their blessings, including their financial blessings, but they will not allow themselves to be reproved by the Word. Wrong thoughts and deceptive teachings have confused them. They won't make a solid decision concerning God's will for their prosperity, and the Word is hindered from working in their spirit and developing them in faith.

What is the difference between a believer who will allow the Word to reprove him and a believer who refuses reproof? Psalm 139:23,24 gives us a clue: **Search me, O God, and know my heart: try me, and know my thoughts: And see if there be any wicked way in me, and lead me in the way everlasting.**

The attitude of the psalmist in these verses is one of humility and reverence. The believer today who holds this attitude will display the same willingness to be reproved by the truth of God's Word. The person will be open and honest in the Presence of the Word and will show reverence toward God when He speaks.

When the Word of God on the subject of wealth is really at work in a person, erroneous teaching and thinking about God's system of wealth will fall by the wayside. The person's thinking will become clear concerning God's will for our wealth, increase, abundance, and overflow. Words that bothered the person in the past, such as "abundance" and "lavishness" will seem normal to him.

Words like abundance and lavishness are words you don't often hear in the Church. The world has taken these words away from the Body of Christ! Yet abundance and great wealth are the believer's spiritual birthright! Abraham, Isaac, Jacob, and others who walked in their covenant with God understood and experienced godly riches and increase. But we as Christians have largely not understood or enjoyed them as we should.

God's assignment to us in this earthly realm is the propagation of His Gospel to the ends of the earth. To fulfill that assignment is going to take stewards who are financially capable of financing this mission. Zechariah 1:17 says, **...Thus saith the Lord of hosts; My cities through prosperity shall yet be spread abroad....** So the increase of God in the earth and the building of His Kingdom shall occur by prosperity. Whose prosperity? The prosperity of those that are His.

Erroneous thinking on the subject of prosperity can only be dismantled by the Word of God proclaimed and revealed by the Holy Ghost. Man can't do it alone by just reading the Bible through lenses of traditional beliefs and indoctrination. But the revelation of the Holy Ghost causes power to be produced when the Bible is read, and that power can tear apart greed, stinginess, selfishness, and fear.

Certain elements of a person's thinking must leave him before he can qualify to walk in divine prosperity. For example, God won't prosper someone abundantly if he or she is stingy. But when a person meets the criterion of desiring to be a blessing, God can trust that person with abundant finances.

Some people are eager to *receive* money, but they don't want to *give* money. But have you ever heard the saying "God can get a blessing *to* you if He can get it *through* you?" It's true. To receive from God, you have to be ready and willing to give to others. You won't be able to handle divine wealth if all you're going to do is "take in" and never "give out." And that working of the Word of God to remove the elements of greed and other hindrances is a work that takes place in the heart and in the mind. For example, Paul wrote in Philippians 4:7, **And the peace of God, which passeth all understanding, shall keep your hearts and minds through Christ Jesus.**

Paul also wrote, **And be not conformed to this world: but be ye transformed by the renewing of your mind, that ye may prove what is that good, and acceptable, and perfect, will of God** (Rom. 12:2). The condition of your mind is so important to God. What you think and believe is paramount when it comes to receiving from God. In fact, the way you think and believe is directly related to the level of blessing you will receive from the Lord.

For example, do you *believe* God's abundance and overflow will come to you every day? Do you *think* every step should be a step of increase? Do you *believe* that now is the time to receive the manifestation of your obedience to tithe and give?

Some people have been tithing for years with no visible signs of significant, supernatural increase. Something needs to be dismantled in their thinking. Their expectation needs to change so the manifestation of those tithes can come through to them.

It seems as if wealth has been sitting over the Church, ready to come down. But the Word of God has to do a work in hearts and minds first before we will be ready to receive those showers of blessings as God intends.

I have pastored for more than thirty years, and I have seen this time and time again. When the anointed Word is brought forth, it brings four things into play as the Scripture says: *doctrine, reproof, correction,* and *instruction* (2 Tim. 3:16). *Doctrine* establishes us in the will of God, and *instruction* shows us how to systematically apply the will of God. But in between becoming established in God's will and then applying His will come *reproof* and *correction.*

When the dismantling power of reproof comes, many believers become offended, thinking they're being wronged somehow. Their attitude is, *I don't have to take this.* They leave and find another church, because their pastor was telling them what they *needed* to hear, but not what they *wanted* to hear. Then they wonder why they're not blessed like they think they should be. It's because they keep running when they're reproved by the Word.

But they *do* have to "take it" if they want to prosper spiritually, physically, financially, and so forth. When the "dismantling" process comes, God is trying to take something out of their lives so He can put something else in their lives in its place: an ability to think clearly—according to the Word of God—so that they can think the thoughts of God.

When you've been reproved, you can receive godly teaching from the Word. If you're not teachable, you're not going to be able to receive from God.

The simple truth is this: *God has already provided for your prosperity. Now you must put yourself in position to receive!*

I sometimes make statements, referring to people who are struggling financially as "broke." I might say things such as, "And you with your 'broke self' can't do anything to further God's Kingdom and His assignment, because you're too far down financially." I say things like that to wake people up, because if I fail to rouse them from their complacency, they will not go any further than they are right now financially.

Yet often they become offended. They're hearing what I'm saying as man talking to man instead of really hearing the Spirit of God in the message. But once they settle down and their anger subsides, their convictions begin to be strengthened. When they know they shouldn't be broke or barely getting by in life, they are on their way to coming out of that situation.

I minister the truth, and when I do, I often cause a stirring. But I'm ministering to people to get results, not applause. If you look at the Old Testament prophets and men and women of God, they went to God's people to carry out God's mission. Jeremiah was commanded by God to root out, tear down, and rebuild (Jer. 1:10). Jeremiah made a lot of enemies, but when a man of God obeys and speaks what God tells Him to speak, it often causes a stirring — a dismantling — and the hearers often feel "cut" as they hear the Word of the Lord.

We already read what Solomon wrote in Ecclesiastes 10:7: **I have seen servants upon horses, and princes walking as servants upon the earth.** And we saw how that is a "backward" situation. In our day, we might word that same verse as follows: "I have seen servants riding in nice cars, and princes riding the bus!"

Just naturally speaking, if a prince doesn't have the where-withal to obtain a horse, he is not likely to be giving away any horses anytime soon. Similarly, if we as believers—as kings and priests unto our God (1 Peter 2:9; Rev. 1:6)—are struggling to have a car of our own, how can we give away cars for the work of ministry?

You see, if I'm operating in the truth of the Word correctly, I will not only have a nice car for my family, I will have the ability to sow a vehicle, or vehicles, into the ministry. If I know how to believe God for a car, I know how to believe Him for one to put in the mission field. That's how our covenant of wealth and our faith for prosperity is supposed to work.

It's difficult to prove out God's goodness to His children when we walk as beggars. A lifestyle of poverty and lack does not reflect the truth that God takes care of His children. In Zechariah 1:15, the Lord said, **And I am very sore displeased with the heathen that are at ease: for I was but a little displeased, and they helped forward the affliction.** In other words, the enemies of God and His people rubbed in God's face, so to speak, the fact that they lived at ease while His children were afflicted.

We also read in Ecclesiastes 10:6, **Folly is set in great dignity, and the rich sit in a low place.** Solomon was observing another backward situation in which folly and foolishness was being dignified.

When we fail to appropriate and enjoy our covenant privileges, our dignity is at stake. In one sense, the dignity of God is at stake, too, because we represent Him. When we have been given so much, yet we are enjoying so little, we need to take a look at how we are representing the Lord. Are we allowing folly to prevail? Could we stand to go further in applying ourselves to receive from Him more effectively?

There are people of God who are hungry for more of God. God wants those people to have the finances so they can have time to read the Word, meditate, and develop themselves spiritually. They need to have the resources—the time and the money—to attend special meetings. They need to have time to be faithful in the church instead of working three jobs. They need to help fund the preaching of the Gospel instead of always trying to scrape together enough money to make ends meet.

When we begin taking our places in Christ and walking in His blessings, dignity will come back to the Church, His Body. For that to happen, we need to be willing to allow reproof to come into our lives through His Word so that we can begin to frame our world financially. May it never be said of us that the traditions of men have made the Word of God of "none effect" in our lives (*see* Mark 7:13).

Number Three: Correction

In review so far, the Word of God that we need to frame our world financially brings to us *doctrine, reproof, correction,* and *instruction in righteousness* (2 Tim. 3:16). We saw that doctrine refers to the established will and order of God. Reproof is the dismantling process in our belief system that must occur so that we may grow strong in our convictions concerning doctrine.

Number three, every believer who wants to change his financial picture must understand *correction.*

"Correction" refers to the inspired assimilation of truth in our thinking that proves out what is the good, acceptable, and perfect will of God (Rom. 12:2).

The Word of God must provide correction in the life of anyone who is truly going to bear fruit spiritually. He has to know for himself what God says about any given subject, whether it's eternal life, healing, or financial, material prosperity. It can't just be his pastor, his spouse, or his friend who knows the truth. He must know the truth before the truth will work for him and produce for him in life.

> **And ye shall know the truth, and the truth shall make you free.**
>
> John 8:32

Notice this verse *doesn't* say, "You shall hear the truth once or twice, and the truth shall make you free." No, you have to *know* the truth before the truth will make a positive difference in your life.

The only way to step into the realm of increase and abundance, where God wants us to abide, is to individually apply ourselves to receiving the Word of God for the purpose of doctrine, reproof, correction, and instruction in righteousness. When we attend to God's Word, allowing the Holy Spirit to reveal God's will, to dismantle wrong beliefs, and to help us assimilate truth, we are going to think differently. We are going to believe differently—and we're going to start talking differently. And life is going to be different for us!

Number Four: Instruction in Righteousness

Number four, every believer who wants to change his financial picture must understand *instruction in righteousness.*

Let's look at "instruction in righteousness" in the light of another verse.

> But whoso looketh into the perfect law of liberty, and continueth therein, he being not a forgetful hearer, but a doer of the work, this man shall be blessed in his deed.
>
> James 1:25

"Instruction in righteousness" refers to the systematic application of God's Word in a person's life. When I say "systematic," I'm talking about a continual, consistent application, not a hit-and-miss treatment of the Word of God.

James 1:25 backs this up: ...**whoso looketh into the perfect law of liberty** [God's Word is "the perfect law of liberty"]**, and continueth therein....** In other words, whoever looks into God's perfect Word and *continues in it* shall be blessed. He will not allow himself to be thrown off-track or off-course by anything that comes, but he is a doer of what he sees in the Word.

Instruction in righteousness also speaks of hearing the Word of righteousness, receiving it, loving it, and obeying it. When you're receiving instruction in righteousness, you're

171

continually adhering to the Word, sticking with it no matter what comes or what anyone else says.

When you know the truth because you've received doctrine, reproof, and correction, and that truth has been applied to your heart, you have instruction that you can walk in. As you walk in it consistently because you're convinced in your heart of the truth and the power of God's Word, you will surely see the fruit of that Word manifested in your life, and you will be blessed in your deeds.

12

How To Frame Your Financial World With the Word of God
Part 2

n the last chapter, we began looking at seven keys to framing our financial world with God's Word. The first four keys— *doctrine, reproof, correction,* and *instruction in righteousness*—come from Second Timothy 3:16. The last three key—*wisdom, understanding,* and *knowledge*—are found in Proverbs 24:3,4, which says,

> Through wisdom is an house builded; and by understanding it is established:
>
> And by knowledge shall the chambers be filled with all precious and pleasant riches.

Number Five: Wisdom

Through wisdom a house is built. We need godly wisdom to build the God-kind of financial wealth in our life. Ecclesiastes 10:10 says, **If the iron be blunt, and he do not whet the edge, then must he put to more strength: but wisdom is profitable to direct.** In other words, without God's wisdom in our finances, we are going to have to put forth more strength and effort to achieve less-than-the-best results. But God doesn't want us to settle for less, because He has provided for us to have the best!

Number five, every believer who wants to change his financial picture must walk in God's *wisdom.*

Wisdom is profitable to direct. Wisdom will even guide your prayer life, such as in the case of Solomon when he became king of Israel. God told him to ask for whatever he wanted, but instead of just asking for money or riches, Solomon asked for wisdom to lead God's people. God granted him wisdom and riches besides (*see* First Kings 3:5-11).

> **Say not thou, What is the cause that the former days were better than these? for thou dost not enquire wisely concerning this.**
>
> **Ecclesiastes 7:10**

When we fail to "inquire wisely," we give place to erroneous teachings and beliefs concerning wealth. And those wrong beliefs can slam doors on people financially and shut them off from receiving revelation from the Bible.

What Is the Cause?

Instead of spending our time wondering why things aren't working financially in our lives as they ought to be working, we should be asking a different kind of question; "Lord, what would You have me do?"

There is a cause, or a reason, for our prosperity, as we have already seen. Our covenant of wealth must be established for the purpose of spreading the Gospel of Christ throughout the earth. When we look at some of the Old Testament patriarchs who were rich, we find that obedience was connected to their prosperity. For example, Abraham heard from God what he was specifically supposed to do, and Abraham obeyed the Lord.

Looking at the life of Solomon, when he became Israel's leader in place of his father David, Solomon didn't ask for riches or honor from the Lord. Instead, he asked God for wisdom to lead God's people. These men and women who prospered at the Lord's hand did so because they found out what God wanted them to do and then did it.

Could obedience to the will of God be wisdom for us today? Yet it seems as if believers today are trying to prosper and obtain wealth any way they can do it—apart from the

Word and the wisdom of God. They're running here and there seeking out ways to get more money in their lives. They're asking the wrong questions. They should be asking the Lord what He would have them do! As it is, they fight rush-hour traffic every day—not to visit the sick, but to try to make a living.

I'm not saying that working is wrong in itself. But I am saying that we shouldn't depend just on our job as our source. Tapping into the wisdom of God must be our source and our confident hope. Then we need to work as unto the Lord and be good stewards of the finances that come in, using our "living" as seed when God calls for it.

As I said, we've been asking the wrong questions. And we've been getting the wrong answers as a result. We've thought the answer was academic. We've thought that we're not prospering as we should because we have the wrong background or the wrong color skin. But it doesn't matter what our background or race, if we will rightly divide the Word of God and give our lives to Him, wisdom from Heaven is available to us, and that wisdom is "profitable to direct." (Eccl. 10:10). In other words, wisdom will get the job done right!

In the last chapter, we looked at James 1:25, which says, **...whoso looketh into the perfect law of liberty, and continueth therein, he being not a forgetful hearer, but a doer of the work, this man shall be blessed in his deed.**

We learned that the "perfect law of liberty" is the Word of God.

Think about it—God's Word would not be the "perfect law of liberty" if it could be changed by someone's background!

We simply can't keep making excuses for our failure in life. If we really want answers, and if we really want change, we have to yield to the works of the Holy Spirit and to the wisdom of God.

I began to prosper financially when I seriously began to hunger and thirst after righteousness (Matt. 5:6) and to eagerly seek God concerning the truth of His Word. I had sat in many services where men of God such as Kenneth E. Hagin, Fred Price and Kenneth Copeland were teaching. I listened to many audio teachings and read many books. I took notes and studied the Word, sometimes throughout the night.

I knew something was missing in my making a connection with God's will and established order for my life. But my question wasn't, "Why am I not prospering?" That would have been the wrong question. I hungered and thirsted for righteousness, and I just wanted to be filled, or satisfied.

Yet how many people have the attitude, I've done better in the past, before I knew about my covenant of wealth? And how many people are trying to get the job done some other way? They're going to night school to further their education, or they're working two jobs. Yet they're still not living as God wants them to live. They can't do very much to fund a missions trip or help provide some other ministry need. Some can't give regularly to support *any* work. And some can't even give their time to usher or help in some other way to make their local church more effective—because their life is consumed with trying to get by in their own strength.

Going by this world's system, you will never have enough money to give like God wants you to give. You will never see God's wealth or live on God's system of prosperity unless you enter the realm of asking the right questions—such as, "What does the wisdom of God say about my prosperity?"

For wisdom is a defence, and money is a defence: but the excellency of knowledge is, that wisdom giveth life to them that have it

Ecclesiastes 7:12

This verse says that **...wisdom is a defence, and money is a defence....** We've already seen that we can't obtain or increase wealth God's way without His wisdom. But right now, I want to look particularly at how money itself can be a defense. Religious people have been saying for years that money is evil. But money in itself is not evil; it's the *love* of money that's evil (1 Tim. 6:10).

What kind of defense is money? It can be a *mortgage* defense, a *utilities* defense, and *groceries* defense, and so forth.

178

Certainly, we praise God for every resource and for the ability to pay our house note and our electric bill and to buy food. But He desires more than that for us. He wants us to have abundant resources. He doesn't want us to be beggars or even to barely skate by in life. Wisdom will have a part in our rising above past circumstances and entering into a new phase of building our lives on the Word of God.

Number Six: Understanding

Number six, every believer who wants to change his financial picture must walk in spiritual *understanding*. Proverbs 24:3 says, **Through wisdom is an house builded; and by understanding it is established.** We need godly understanding of financial matters in order to become established in God's covenant of wealth in our lives.

There is a godly understanding that we need to tap into, but there is also a natural, human understanding. Let's look at another couple of verses that talks about "understanding."

Trust in the Lord with all thine heart; and lean not unto thine own understanding.

In all thy ways acknowledge him, and he shall direct thy paths.

Proverbs 3:5,6

In finances as well as anything else in life, the believer has to have the understanding of God in order to believe and trust Him. Then once the person enters into that realm of trusting and believing God, he must not lean to his own understanding, but to God's. In other words, the person who trusts God must not swerve or sway from His dependency on God and His Word no matter what line of human or devilish reasoning is presented to his mind.

Trust and Obey

In John 2:5 when the hosts of "the wedding at Cana" ran out of wine, Mary told the servants at the wedding, **...Whatsoever he [Jesus] saith unto you, do it.** Jesus has done so many miraculous things with just our obedience and willingness. We must simply trust and obey instead of leaning to our own understanding.

Leaning to our own understanding has also led many of us into generational traps and has imprisoned us in our own minds—in our own thinking. We often lean on family history or to failures of the past instead of on the truth of God's Word that says we are new creatures in Christ and joint-heirs of God with Jesus (2 Cor. 5:17; Rom. 8:17). We should understand that certain blessings belong to us by virtue of our union with Him. Instead, we have allowed our own wrong thinking to rob us.

Third John 2 says, **Beloved, I wish above all things that thou mayest prosper and be in health, even as thy soul**

prospereth. Don't concentrate on debt anymore, but concentrate on prosperity. Do whatever you have to do to change your mindset about money. Get hold of some good books on the subject of prosperity. Search out and study every verse you can find. Instead of making more debt, lock yourself away with the Word and with some good Word teachings on prosperity. Get a word from God about your finances and then don't turn from it *ever.* Pay the price to do what it takes to cause your soul to prosper because it's so full of and established on the Word.

God is waiting for you to act. The day can come when you will no longer have to borrow a dime, and you can live in whatever kind of house you want. As I said before, hovering over the Body of Christ is all the goodness of God waiting for a channel through which to travel. All God needs is someone to open his heart and mind and let it in. So give Him your unswerving faith and trust, and refuse to lean to your own understanding.

The person who's full of faith chooses to believe what God says over anything he can feel or see. He makes the decision to believe, and all debating about it is over. He is now on a spiritual journey—a successful, prosperous journey. His spirit begins drawing and pulling toward himself what he is believing and saying. His heart grows stronger, and his mind grows clearer. He begins to think, believe, and say better and better things about his situation and his life. And things begin to change for the better and work out for his good.

The "faith message" has received a lot of criticism in the Body of Christ. But there is a true faith message, because the Bible says, "The just shall live by faith" (Rom. 1:17; Gal. 3:11; Heb. 10:38). When a person believes and says what God's Word says about a situation, faith makes the connection that enables that person to receive from God.

Number Seven: Knowledge

Number seven, every believer who wants to change his financial picture must walk in revelation *knowledge*.

You can't believe, or have faith, beyond actual knowledge. That's why Paul wrote, **So then faith cometh by hearing, and hearing by the word of God** (Rom. 10:17).

The Bible also says we are destroyed because of lack of knowledge (Hos. 4:6). We cannot receive covenant wealth from God without revelation knowledge of the truth of His Word on the subject.

First Corinthians 2:9,10 says,

But as it is written, Eye hath not seen, nor ear heard, neither have entered into the heart of man, the things which God hath prepared for them that love him.

But God hath revealed them unto us by his Spirit: for the Spirit searcheth all things, yea, the deep things of God.

God is constantly revealing the good things He has prepared for those who love Him. The more we seek Him, the more revelation knowledge we'll receive from the Word about those good things.

My own knowledge of God's Word has increased over the years. I am fully convinced of the will of God for our prosperity—our financial well-being—because I have studied the Bible on the subject. But even in my young adulthood, I knew something was wrong in the church concerning financial wealth; I just didn't know what to do about it.

When I came out of the world into the Body of Christ, I observed that the world in large part has no problem with *living* in the best, *driving* the best, *wearing* the best, and so forth. But in many of the local churches I attended, I saw a beggarly spirit.

Since I hadn't had any teaching on the subject, I began to think these Christians' attitude toward money was appropriate. I had never heard anything else, so that's what I began to believe too. And I began to "perish" financially because of my lack of knowledge. I couldn't have faith for finances, because I hadn't heard the Word of God on the subject. I couldn't believe beyond my knowledge of the truth.

Jesus set up a whole new system for the Church to live by. We've been grieving the Father trying to get by on the world's system. But we have begun to see the light. So what are we waiting for? It's time to frame our world for prosperity according to the will and plan of God.

What Are You Waiting For?
Begin *Now* To Frame Your Financial World!

In framing your financial world with the Word of God, these seven factors we looked at must come into play. By way of review, they are as follows:

1. Doctrine	5. Wisdom
2. Reproof	6. Understanding
3. Correction	7. Knowledge
4. Instruction in Righteousness	

To walk in divine prosperity, you must have the Word of God working in your life to bring *doctrine, reproof, correction, instruction in righteousness, wisdom, understanding,* and *knowledge.* As we saw in the beginning of Chapter 11, framing your financial world entails laying the proper foundation, providing the framework for that which you're building, and then adding the finishing touches.

In short, framing your world with God's Word is fashioning your life after God's pattern and design. In stands to reason you would need to know God's pattern, or blueprint, in order to build successfully.

God has given us His pattern throughout the pages of His Book, the Bible. It's not the world's pattern, but God's. And operating within God's pattern requires action on our part regarding the seven keys, or factors, we just studied.

Abraham operated according to that pattern. He left his comfortable surroundings behind and headed for place that God would later show him (Gen. 12:1). In other words, when Abraham obeyed God and left, he didn't even know where he was going! And we can see that Isaac operated according to that pattern when he sowed in famine, yet received a hundred-fold return on his sowing (Gen. 26:12). But they couldn't have done it had they not passed God's test of faith, obedience, and complete trust.

Evidence of a Life 'Well-Framed'

We know that framing your world with God's Word is fashioning your life after God's pattern. When we're just beginning to frame our world, we may not see the beautiful framework of God's design at first. But we will see it, because when we begin framing our world with the Word of God, God sets us on a sure course. God is unchangeable, and His Word is infallible. More and more, as we frame our financial world with God's Word, there will be certain signs, or evidence, of the change that has taken place.

What are some of those signs?

Order as a Sign

Number one, there will be a certain order to your life. Finances play a big part in the order of your life, because when your finances aren't in order, it affects almost every other area of your life too.

I've been broke in life, but now I am wealthy. And I don't know about you, but I even pray better wealthy! Just as my lack affected every area of my life, my prosperity also affects every area of my life. I don't have to deal with certain distractions like I used to, because I paid the price to order my life after God's pattern and design. God desires this "framework" to be evident in the life of every one of His children.

Contentment as a Sign

Number two, along with order, you will have a certain sense of rest and contentment in your life when your financial world has been framed by the Word of God. Job 22:21 (*NIV*) says, **Submit to God and be at peace with him; in this way prosperity will come to you. There is a blessedness to yielding to God and to the truth of His Word.**

Everyone in life, whether sinner or saint, is searching for a greater sense of contentment. Yet contentment seems to elude so many because they are not yielded to God. There are many reasons why: lack of knowledge, lack of understanding, lack of wisdom, and so forth. Many have been brought up in churches that believe the prosperity message is wrong—that it's carnal or even sinful. Some of these people simply refuse to be open to the truth. Other people have encountered so much hardship and loss, and they've allowed themselves to become bitter. They haven't understood that God is not their enemy—that when things go wrong in a person's life, God desires to prepare a table of provision and blessing—right in the presence of the enemy (Ps. 23:5)!

God is for you, not against you. So don't set yourself against Him. Setting yourself against the Lord is a losing proposition, anyway. So forget about all the bad things that have happened. Submit to God and be at peace so He can bring about the good in your life that He desires to bring.

In Psalm 23, right after it says, **Thou preparest a table before me in the presence of mine enemies...**, it also says, **...thou anointest my head with oil; my cup runneth over** (v. 5). This psalm is a beautiful hymn of redemption and grace, not a funeral dirge as many have believed. I encourage you to read the entire Psalm, because it paints a vivid picture of who Jesus the Shepherd is to us today!

Teaching Corrects Error

So much of the tension and unrest in the Body of Christ today is due to a lack of finances. Teaching can correct the problem. Christians must rise up and take responsibility for walking in the blessings of God that He has already provided for. But because there has been error and excess in the Body of Christ, Satan deceives many into rejecting the teaching and into being timid or confused about money. Many of these believers are sincere, goodhearted people. They are simply being robbed of the life of peace, rest, and contentment that God wants them to live.

Empowerment as a Sign

Number three, besides order and contentment, a person who has framed his financial world with God's Word will be empowered. He or she will be equipped and in position to help fund the propagation of the Gospel in a significant way.

It's a sad day when believers yearn to give toward furthering the Gospel and the Kingdom of God, but they are so strapped making a house payment, two car payments, and payments to credit card companies that they can't give big to the funding of the Gospel.

Certainly, everyone should do his or her part in giving toward spreading the Good News, but not everyone does. The enemy has tried to squeeze the life out of the Gospel, so to speak, by trying to keep it one little corner. The devil trembles with fear at the prospect of the Gospel being thrust beyond the four walls of our home, our church, or even our community. So he has people thinking constantly about "*their* things—*their* house, *their* cars, their boats, *their* good time." God wants to bless them lavishly, but people have been blessing themselves on credit, and they're too broke to keep up with their lifestyle, much less support a ministry or a missionary.

We are commanded to "go into all the world and preach the Gospel" (Mark 16:15). Do we think people travel to or live in other countries for free? No, it takes finances to get the job done. We've been too busy believing "all that preacher wants is my money" to notice the forces of darkness at work against the Gospel. And one of the big hindrances is money.

But when a child of God frames his financial world with the Word of God, "money cometh" to him or her for the purpose of empowerment! That person understands that if the bars and casinos in the world can be first-class, the local church can certainly be first-class! He won't be trying to keep the preacher poor, because He knows the nature and character of God. He won't be stingy or greedy because He has a heart for souls and desires with all of his heart to see people delivered from sin, bondage, and tradition. He is concerned about others, not just himself or his family.

When you can look beyond the four walls of your world and reach out to help make a better life for others, you are truly an empowered man or woman of God in the Body of Christ.

We can see that there are many reasons to diligently apply ourselves to the framing of our financial world with God's Word, all of them rich and rewarding because that's the kind of God we serve—One who produces order, contentment, and empowerment in the lives of those who follow Him completely.

Divine Sequence: The Pathway to Blessing

As we saw in Chapter 1, the ABC's of how to frame your world with the Word of God refer to a person's thinking right, believing right, and speaking right — in that order. In other words, you must think right (in line with the Word of God) in order to believe right (in line with the Word of God). And you must believe right to speak right (in line with the Word of God).

The following is a word I recently received from the Lord.

You are a thinking spirit.

You are a believing spirit.

And you are a speaking spirit.

My Word says in Ephesians 4:23

That you are to be renewed in the spirit of your mind.

And Scripture also says that you are to believe with your spirit.

You are a thinking spirit.

You are a believing spirit.

And you are a speaking spirit.

The Word of God has to get your *thinking,* your *believing,* and your *speaking straight* whether you're believing for healing, deliverance, prosperity, restoration, or *anything* God's Word promises. So you must follow the ABC's for framing your financial world in the same way you would follow the pattern to frame any area of your life to conform to the Word and the will of God.

Notice there is an order, or sequence, in receiving from God—much like there is order in our alphabet: "A" comes before "B," and "B" comes before "C," and so forth. Receiving from God and changing your life to one of blessing, joy, peace, and contentment begin first and foremost with your thoughts.

A. You Must 'Think Right' Concerning Covenant Wealth

Your thoughts are more powerful than you may realize. Second Corinthians 10:5 says, **Casting down imaginations, and every high thing that exalteth itself against the**

knowledge of God, and bringing into captivity every thought to the obedience of Christ.

Imaginations are high, lofty reasonings and arguments that exalt themselves against the truth of God's Word. They come against us for a reason: to hold us back and to keep us in want. Wrong thinking—thinking thoughts that are contrary to God's Word—will rob us of faith and victory. That's why Paul was inspired by the Holy Ghost to show us how to deal with wrong thoughts. We're to cast them down, bringing them under the dominion and authority of God's holy, written, unchanging Word.

Philippians 2:5 says, **Let this mind be in you, which was also in Christ Jesus.** That means we must allow the mind of Christ to have the uppermost place of dominion and authority in our mind. Well, what mind was in Christ Jesus? He revealed what was on His mind in His earthly ministry, and He continued to reveal Himself through the Holy Spirit after His resurrection. But for the purpose of this teaching, let's look at just a few facts about our Lord concerning prosperity while He walked on the earth.

1. **Nobles brought treasures to Jesus even when He was a Babe in a manger.**

2. **A woman lavished expensive perfume on Jesus' feet, and He did not rebuke her.**

3. Jesus and His disciples had a treasury as they traveled and ministered, and one of His disciples was specifically assigned to handle the group's finances.

4. Jesus had associations with the rich.

5. Jesus never scorned people just because they were wealthy.

6. Jesus fed multitudes—some 5,000 people—with five loaves and two fish.

7. A fisherman's net broke because it was too full of fish — although Peter had fished all night in vain, at Jesus' command, he cast out his net one more time, and abundance ensued.

8. Jesus received money to pay His taxes—and Peter's—from the mouth of a fish.

9. Jesus rode into Jerusalem on a donkey that had never been ridden before—not a used, second-hand mode of transportation.

10. Jesus' garments were valuable enough to be used as stakes by the Roman soldiers who gambled for possession of them.

11. Jesus was buried in a rich man's tomb.

12. Jesus was present at the Creation of all things. The earth is His and the fullness thereof, and all things were and are at His disposal.

Jesus was the express will of the Father in the earth. We must follow His example and change our thinking concerning prosperity if we are going to properly express the will of God in the earth.

You've probably heard the saying, in effect, "Your *choices* will determine your *habits*; your *habits* will determine your *lifestyle*; and your *lifestyle* will determine your *destiny*."

Similarly, your *thoughts* will determine your *believing*; your *believing* will determine your *speaking*; and your *speaking* will determine not only *the level of blessing you will receive from God in life*, but it will also set your destiny *on a determined, godly course*.

Your thoughts will affect how you believe and how you speak, or how you act on what you believe. Thoughts are powerful! They can set off a chain-reaction of behavior that will ultimately bring blessing or cursing to your life. That's why Paul exhorted us to pray, to refrain from anxiety, and to allow God's peace to guard our heart and our mind (Phil. 4:6,7).

How To Make a Change

In order to change the way you think, you must choose to think something different. For example, if you have been thinking that you'll never get ahead financially, you need to start thinking, **I am the head and not the tail—above only and not beneath. Jesus became poor that I might be rich. God delights in my prosperity** (Deut. 28:13; 2 Cor. 8:9; Ps. 35:27). Then begin thinking those right thoughts over and over and over again until they become "second nature" to you. In other words, without consciously choosing to think those thoughts, those thoughts will "pop up" in your mind, because they have become a part of you. Those thoughts will become lodged deep within your heart.

God's Word will change your mind, because you were born again by the powerful, incorruptible seed of the Word of God (1 Peter 1:23). God's Word has a renewing capacity and a quickening capacity, because the Word is Spirit and life (John 6:63). When you yield to them, God's Word and His thoughts will begin to produce something alive in your spirit. Instead of thinking lack, you'll think abundance. Instead of thinking *subtraction*, you'll think *addition*. Then instead of thinking *addition*, you'll think *multiplication*. And instead of thinking *when*, you'll think *now!*

B. You Must 'Believe Right' Concerning Covenant Wealth

Hebrews 11:6 says, **But without faith it is impossible to please him: for he that cometh to God must believe that he is, and that he is a rewarder of them that diligently**

seek him. How important is our faith, then? It is of paramount importance.

Being faithless and refusing God's abundance was the problem the Israelites had in the wilderness. Instead of believing God and marching right in by faith to take their Promised Land, they moaned and complained about their circumstances and lack.

Read carefully the following verses from Hebrews 3:7-10 that talk about the seriousness of unbelief.

Wherefore (as the Holy Ghost saith, To day if ye will hear his voice,

Harden not your hearts, as in the provocation, in the day of temptation in the wilderness:

When your fathers tempted me, proved me, and saw my works forty years.

Wherefore I was grieved with that generation, and said, They do alway err in their heart [to disbelieve is to err]; and they have not known my ways.

So I sware in my wrath, They shall not enter into my rest.)

Take heed, brethren, lest there be in any of you an evil heart of unbelief, in departing from the living God.

But exhort one another daily, while it is called To day; lest any of you be hardened through the deceitfulness of sin.

> For we are made partakers of Christ, if we hold the beginning of our confidence stedfast unto the end;
>
> While it is said, To day if ye will hear his voice, harden not your hearts, as in the provocation.
>
> For some, when they had heard, did provoke: howbeit not all that came out of Egypt by Moses.
>
> But with whom was he grieved forty years? was it not with them that had sinned [unbelief is sin], whose carcases fell in the wilderness?
>
> And to whom sware he that they should not enter into his rest, but to them that believed not?
>
> So we see that they could not enter in because of unbelief.

God was put out with the children of Israel for what He called "an evil heart of unbelief" (v. 12). And because of their unbelief, they could not enter into the blessing He had already provided for them and had already said was theirs.

What is unbelief? According to the Bible, unbelief is not non-belief, but it is believing something other than what God's Word says. This kind of unbelief is also the same as being unpersuadable. The children of Israel refused to be persuaded that God had set before them a beautiful future filled with prosperity and contentment. And in the process of refusing to believe God, they were, in effect, refusing God Himself as well as His promise to them. They "departed from the Living God" (*see* Hebrews 3:12).

God called unbelief evil in the Old Testament, and He calls unbelief evil today. Notice again that Hebrews 3:12 says, **Take heed, brethren, lest there be in any of you an evil heart of unbelief, in departing from the living God.**

Let's look more in-depth at the unbelief of the Israelites. As we saw in Chapter 8, when God first talked to Moses about giving the Israelites the Promised Land, Moses sent twelve spies, one from each of the twelve tribes of Israel, to spy out the land and to bring back a report. When the twelve returned, all but two of them gave an evil report. The ten spies reported to Moses,

...We came unto the land whither thou sentest us, and surely it floweth with milk and honey; and this is the fruit of it.

Nevertheless the people be strong that dwell in the land, and the cities are walled, and very great: and moreover we saw the children of Anak there.

...The land, through which we have gone to search it, is a land that eateth up the inhabitants thereof; and all the people that we saw in it are men of a great stature.

And there we saw the giants, the sons of Anak, which come of the giants: and we were in our own sight as grasshoppers, and so we were in their sight.

Numbers 13:27, 28, 32, 33

Only two of the twelve, Caleb and Joshua, brought back a faith-filled report. The other spies were complaining: **The**

Amalekites dwell in the land of the south: and the Hittites, and the Jebusites, and the Amorites, dwell in the mountains: and the Canaanites dwell by the sea, and by the coast of Jordan (v. 29).

But look at how Caleb responded.

And Caleb stilled the people before Moses, and said, Let us go up at once, and possess it; for we are well able to overcome it.

Numbers 13:30

Instead of allowing what Caleb said to reprove them and dismantle the stronghold of unbelief within them, the ten spies reacted with still more unbelief.

Numbers 13:31,32 says,

But the men that went up with him said, We be not able to go up against the people; for they are stronger than we.

And they brought up an evil report....

At Moses' request, God pardoned the sin of the people, but He swore that the generation of those who brought back the evil report of unbelief would never see the Promised Land.

The Lord made an exception, saying, But my servant Caleb, because he had another spirit with him, and hath followed me fully, him will I bring into the land whereinto he went; and his seed shall possess it (Num. 14:24).

And the men, which Moses sent to search the land, who returned, and made all the congregation to murmur against him, by bringing up a slander upon the land,

Even those men that did bring up the evil report upon the land, died by the plague before the Lord.

But Joshua the son of Nun, and Caleb the son of Jephunneh, which were of the men that went to search the land, lived still.

Numbers 14:36-38

Moses endured the Israelites' unbelief in the wilderness. Like Joshua and Caleb, Moses fully believed in God's promise. Moses understood prosperity because he grew up in Pharaoh's household. I believe God used Moses' background to prepare him to lead his people out of Egypt and to the Promised Land.

It is important to note that the Israelites didn't get into trouble in the wilderness because they asked for too much; they got into trouble with God because they wouldn't accept His promise of abundance by faith. Twelve men saw the fruitful land God was giving them, but only two believed it. The others refused God's promises, and they influenced an entire generation to do the same.

You can't frame your financial world after the pattern of prosperity if you're doubting God's will and provision in the matter. You can't enter in to the realm of living in covenant wealth if you are at the same time refusing it. You must think right according to God's holy Word, and you must believe right concerning what He has spoken, because He is faithful who promised (Heb. 10:23).

C. You Must 'Speak Right' Concerning Covenant Wealth

I once heard a wise minister say, in effect "If we want the God-kind of results, we're going to have to find out how God works and work with Him." God operates by speaking forth faith-filled words. At least nine times in Genesis, it says, "And God *said*." And what God said came to pass. For example, in Genesis 1:3 we read, **And God said, Let there be light: and there was light.**

Similarly, we must speak the living Word over our lives, including over our finances. Jesus said, **Have the faith of God** (Mark 11:22). A more literal translation of that verse reads, "Have the God-kind of faith." The Apostle Paul wrote in Ephesians 5:1, **Be ye therefore followers** [imitators] **of God, as dear children.** And as children of God, we frame our world the same way God framed the world in the beginning: by speaking *words*.

By the same method of speaking words of faith as God did at Creation, you as a believer can create in your life the things that you want—the things God wants you to have and says you can have.

Jesus was the absolute portrait of a Man of faith, who abided in God and kept God's Word in His heart and mouth. Jesus was so developed in speaking words of faith that He changed circumstances and lives everywhere He went.

We have kept Jesus in a category all by Himself. Certainly, He is God—the only Savior and Redeemer of man. But when He walked the earth, He was also setting an example for us to live by. We can't imitate His great substitutionary act, but we *should* imitate His example!

Christians have been robbed of financial success because they have been framing their world with the wrong words. Perhaps it's because of ignorance; they don't understand that God delights in their prosperity. But the truth remains that death and life are in the power of the tongue: and they that love it shall eat the fruit thereof (Prov. 18:21).

You need to get the words, "I can't afford" out of your vocabulary. There is no such thing with God! The next time you see something you want, instead of saying, "I can't afford this," tell whatever it is, "I'll be back!"

We already looked at Hebrews 3:7-10 concerning the sin of unbelief. Now let's back up to Hebrews 3:1:

> Wherefore, holy brethren, partakers of the heavenly
> calling, consider the Apostle and High Priest of our profession,
> Christ Jesus.

Notice that word "profession." One meaning of the word "profess" means, in effect, *to acknowledge or to say the same as*. In other words, to profess something means to say, or confess, something. This verse says that Jesus Christ is the Apostle and High Priest of our profession. He is the High Priest of our confession—of our saying the same thing He says. When we get to the point where we're always thinking Christ's thoughts and saying His words, or saying the same thing He says, we will get the same results—manifestations of His Word in power!

The Expansiveness of God

No one but you can hold back the blessings of God from your life. So be a radical Christian and just do what God wants you to do! Follow the ABC's of framing your financial world through right *thinking*, right *believing*, and right *speaking*.

God is about blessing and increase, not cursing and decrease. But are we willing to pay the price to walk in the expansiveness of God?

When we walk by faith, everything that happens on the outside begins on the inside, in our spirit. When we learn how to operate and function from the inside out, we will increase with the increase of God. Job 8:7 says, **Though thy beginning was small, yet thy latter end should greatly increase.** Will we attend to God's Word continually so that it begins to affect every area of our life—our thinking, our believing, and our speaking?

I encourage you to speak forth God's enlargement and expansion in your life. You have a right to use His words with authority. I dare you to boldly declare, "Nothing but the best is going to happen today!" and then live your life holding to that mindset. Those words will produce faith in your heart — a brand-new belief system — and those words will eventually produce the reality of what you've been saying.

How To Tap Into the Spirit

There is one last factor framing for your financial world with God's Word or to receiving *any* blessing from the Word. It encompasses each of the ABC's of the framing process — *thinking, believing,* and *speaking.* What is this factor? *Thanksgiving,* or *the giving of thanks unto God.*

In the account of the prodigal son in Luke 15, when the wandering son returned to his father's house, the elder son became angry with his father for celebrating a "scoundrel's" homecoming. The father was willing and eager to bless his younger son, whom his big brother deemed as unworthy and undeserving. As the father was preparing for the festivities, the older brother said to his father, in effect, "I've been here this entire time. I didn't leave you, yet you've never done anything like this for me" (Luke 15:29).

The father responded to his angry son, **...Son, thou art ever with me, and all that I have is thine** (v. 31). In essence, the father was saying, "You could have had a party anytime. Everything I have is at your disposal."

This older son did not recognize how blessed he was in his father's house. Therefore, he couldn't appreciate those blessings the way the younger son learned to appreciate them.

Similarly, we must show devout gratitude to God for all the blessings that are at our disposal — the blessings that are ours to the extent we recognize and accept them.

Many believers today are simply unappreciative of the many great things God has done for them through Christ's death, burial, and resurrection. They don't know that one of the quickest ways to walk in the Spirit and tap into the riches of God is with a spirit of deep gratitude.

Each one of us can find something to be thankful for! First and foremost, we can thank God for the sacrifice of the Cross and the power and blessing that came into our lives as a result of Jesus' sacrificial act.

I encourage you to open your heart and mind to the possibilities of God within you. As you hunger and thirst after God's righteousness and after His way of doing things, you will begin

Prayer of Salvation

A born-again, committed relationship with God is the key to the victorious life. Jesus, the Son of God, laid down His life and rose again so that we could spend eternity with Him in heaven and experience His absolute best on earth. The Bible says, **For God so loved the world, that he gave his only begotten Son, that whosoever believeth in him should not perish, but have everlasting life** (John 3:16).

It is the will of God that everyone receive eternal salvation. The way to receive this salvation is to call upon the name of Jesus and confess Him as your Lord. The Bible says, **That if thou shalt confess with thy mouth the Lord Jesus, and shalt believe in thine heart that God hath raised him from the dead, thou shalt be saved. For whosoever shall call upon the name of the Lord shall be saved** (Romans 10:9-10,13).

Jesus has given salvation, healing and countless benefits to all who call upon His name. These benefits can be yours if you receive Him into your heart by praying this prayer:

Father God,

I come to you right now as a sinner. Right now, I choose to turn away from sin, and I ask you to cleanse me of all unrighteousness. I believe that your Son, Jesus, died on the cross to take away my sins. I also believe that He rose again from the dead so that I might be justified and made righteous through faith in Him. I call upon the name of Jesus Christ for salvation. I want Him to be the Savior and Lord of my life. Jesus, I choose to follow You, and ask that You fill me with the power of the Holy Spirit. I declare that right now, I am a born-again child of God. I am free from sin, and full of the righteousness of God. I am saved in Jesus' Name, Amen.

If you have prayed this prayer to receive Jesus Christ into your life, we would like to hear from you. Please write us at:

Ever Increasing Word Ministries
P.O. Box 7
Darrow, LA 70725

About the Author

D
r. **Leroy Thompson, Sr.** is the pastor and founder of Word of Life Christian Center in Darrow, Louisiana, a growing and thriving body of believers from various walks of life. He has been in the ministry since 1973, serving as a pastor since 1976. Even though he completed his undergraduate degree and theology doctorate and was an instructor for several years at a Christian Bible college in Louisiana, it wasn't until 1983, when he received the baptism in the Holy Spirit, that the revelation knowledge of God's Word changed his life; and it continues to increase his ministry. Dr. Thompson attributes the success of his life and ministry to his reliance on the Word of God, being filled with the Holy Spirit and being led by the Spirit of God. Today Dr. Thompson travels across the United States taking the message of ministerial excellence, dedication and discipline to the body of Christ.

To contact Dr. Leroy Thompson, Sr.,

write:

Dr. Leroy Thompson, Sr.

Ever Increasing Word Ministries

P.O. Box 7

Darrow, Louisiana 70725

*Please include your prayer requests
and comments when you write.*